Layers of Learning

Year Two • Unit One

Byzantines
Turkey
Climate & Seasons
Byzantine Art

Published by HooDoo Publishing
United States of America
© 2014 Layers of Learning
Copies of maps or activities may be made for a particular family or classroom.
ISBN 978-1495294884

If you wish to reproduce or print excerpts of this publication, please contact us at contact@layers-of-learning.com for permission. Thank you for respecting copyright laws.

Units At A Glance: Topics For All Four Years of the Layers of Learning Program

1	History	Geography	Science	The Arts
1	Mesopotamia	Maps & Globes	Planets	Cave Paintings
2	Egypt	Map Keys	Stars	Egyptian Art
3	Europe	Global Grids	Earth & Moon	Crafts
4	Ancient Greece	Wonders	Satellites	Greek Art
5	Babylon	Mapping People	Humans in Space	Poetry
6	The Levant	Physical Earth	Laws of Motion	List Poems
7	Phoenicians	Oceans	Motion	Moral Stories
8	Assyrians	Deserts	Fluids	Rhythm
9	Persians	Arctic	Waves	Melody
10	Ancient China	Forests	Machines	Chinese Art
11	Early Japan	Mountains	States of Matter	Line & Shape
12	Arabia	Rivers & Lakes	Atoms	Color & Value
13	Ancient India	Grasslands	Elements	Texture & Form
14	Ancient Africa	Africa	Bonding	African Tales
15	First North Americans	North America	Salts	Creative Kids
16	Ancient South America	South America	Plants	South American Art
17	Celts	Europe	Flowering Plants	Jewelry
18	Roman Republic	Asia	Trees	Roman Art
19	Christianity	Australia & Oceania	Simple Plants	Instruments
20	Roman Empire	You Explore	Fungi	Composing Music

2	History	Geography	Science	The Arts
1	Byzantines	Turkey	Climate & Seasons	Byzantine Art
2	Barbarians	Ireland	Forecasting	Illumination
3	Islam	Arabian Peninsula	Clouds & Precipitation	Creative Kids
4	Vikings	Norway	Special Effects	Viking Art
5	Anglo Saxons	Britain	Wild Weather	King Arthur Tales
6	Charlemagne	France	Cells and DNA	Carolingian Art
7	Normans	Nigeria	Skeletons	Canterbury Tales
8	Feudal System	Germany	Muscles, Skin, & Cardiopulmonary	Gothic Art
9	Crusades	Balkans	Digestive & Senses	Religious Art
10	Burgundy, Venice, Spain	Switzerland	Nerves	Oil Paints
11	Wars of the Roses	Russia	Health	Minstrels & Plays
12	Eastern Europe	Hungary	Metals	Printmaking
13	African Kingdoms	Mali	Carbon Chem	Textiles
14	Asian Kingdoms	Southeast Asia	Non-metals	Vivid Language
15	Mongols	Caucasus	Gases	Fun With Poetry
16	Medieval China & Japan	China	Electricity	Asian Arts
17	Pacific Peoples	Micronesia	Circuits	Arts of the Islands
18	American Peoples	Canada	Technology	Indian Legends
19	The Renaissance	Italy	Magnetism	Renaissance Art I
20	Explorers	Caribbean Sea	Motors	Renaissance Art II

3	History	Geography	Science	The Arts
1	Age of Exploration	Argentina and Chile	Classification & Insects	Fairy Tales
2	The Ottoman Empire	Egypt and Libya	Reptiles & Amphibians	Poetry
3	Mogul Empire	Pakistan & Afghanistan	Fish	Mogul Arts
4	Reformation	Angola & Zambia	Birds	Reformation Art
5	Renaissance England	Tanzania & Kenya	Mammals & Primates	Shakespeare
6	Thirty Years' War	Spain	Sound	Baroque Music
7	The Dutch	Netherlands	Light & Optics	Baroque Art I
8	France	Indonesia	Bending Light	Baroque Art II
9	The Enlightenment	Korean Pen.	Color	Art Journaling
10	Russia & Prussia	Central Asia	History of Science	Watercolors
11	Conquistadors	Baltic States	Igneous Rocks	Creative Kids
12	Settlers	Peru & Bolivia	Sedimentary Rocks	Native American Art
13	13 Colonies	Central America	Metamorphic Rocks	Settler Sayings
14	Slave Trade	Brazil	Gems & Minerals	Colonial Art
15	The South Pacific	Australasia	Fossils	Principles of Art
16	The British in India	India	Chemical Reactions	Classical Music
17	Boston Tea Party	Japan	Reversible Reactions	Folk Music
18	Founding Fathers	Iran	Compounds & Solutions	Rococo
19	Declaring Independence	Samoa and Tonga	Oxidation & Reduction	Creative Crafts I
20	The American Revolution	South Africa	Acids & Bases	Creative Crafts II

4	History	Geography	Science	The Arts
1	American Government	USA	Heat & Temperature	Patriotic Music
2	Expanding Nation	Pacific States	Motors & Engines	Tall Tales
3	Industrial Revolution	U.S. Landscapes	Energy	Romantic Art I
4	Revolutions	Mountain West States	Energy Sources	Romantic Art II
5	Africa	U.S. Political Maps	Energy Conversion	Impressionism I
6	The West	Southwest States	Earth Structure	Impressionism II
7	Civil War	National Parks	Plate Tectonics	Post-Impressionism
8	World War I	Plains States	Earthquakes	Expressionism
9	Totalitarianism	U.S. Economics	Volcanoes	Abstract Art
10	Great Depression	Heartland States	Mountain Building	Kinds of Art
11	World War II	Symbols and Landmarks	Chemistry of Air & Water	War Art
12	Modern East Asia	The South States	Food Chemistry	Modern Art
13	India's Independence	People of America	Industry	Pop Art
14	Israel	Appalachian States	Chemistry of Farming	Modern Music
15	Cold War	U.S. Territories	Chemistry of Medicine	Free Verse
16	Vietnam War	Atlantic States	Food Chains	Photography
17	Latin America	New England States	Animal Groups	Latin American Art
18	Civil Rights	Home State Study	Instincts	Theater & Film
19	Technology	Home State Study II	Habitats	Architecture
20	Terrorism	America in Review	Conservation	Creative Kids

Unit 2-1 Printable Pack

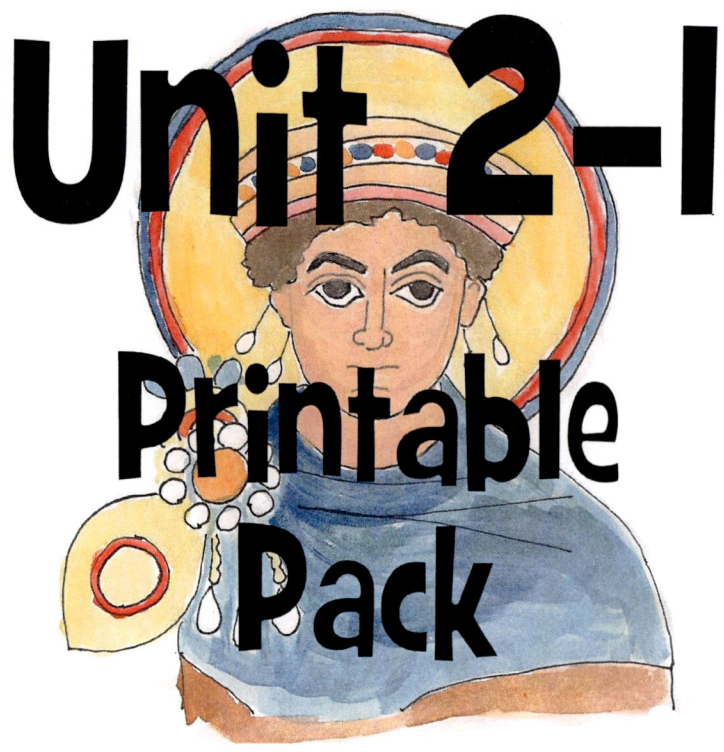

This unit includes printables at the end. To make life easier for you we also created digital printable packs for each unit. To retrieve your printable pack for Unit 2-1, please visit

www.layers-of-learning.com/digital-printable-packs/

Put the printable pack in your shopping cart and use this coupon code:

0121UNIT2-1

Your printable pack will be free.

LAYERS OF LEARNING INTRODUCTION

This is part of a series of units in the Layers of Learning homeschool curriculum, including the subjects of history, geography, science, and the arts. Children from 1st through 12th can participate in the same curriculum at the same time – family school style.

The units are intended to be used in order as the basis of a complete curriculum (once you add in a systematic math, reading, and writing program). You begin with Year 1 Unit 1 no matter what ages your children are. Spend about 2 weeks on each unit. You pick and choose the activities within the unit that appeal to you and read the books from the book list that are available to you or find others on the same topic from your library. We highly recommend that you use the timeline in every history section as the backbone. Then flesh out your learning with reading and activities that highlight the topics you think are the most important.

Alternatively, you can use the units as activity ideas to supplement another curriculum in any order you wish. You can still use them with all ages of children at the same time.

When you've finished with Year One, move on to Year Two, Year Three, and Year Four. Then begin again with Year One and work your way through the years again. Now your children will be older, reading more involved books, and writing more in depth. When you have completed the sequence for the second time, you start again on it for the third and final time. If your student began with Layers of Learning in 1st grade and stayed with it all the way through she would go through the four year rotation three times, firmly cementing the information in her mind in ever increasing depth. At each level you should expect increasing amounts of outside reading and writing. High schoolers in particular should be reading extensively, and if possible, participating in discussion groups.

☺ ☺ ☺ These icons will guide you in spotting activities and books that are appropriate for the age of child you are working with. But if you think an activity is too juvenile or too difficult for your kids, adjust accordingly. The icons are not there as rules, just guides.

☺ GRADES 1-4
☺ GRADES 5-8
☺ GRADES 9-12

Within each unit we share:
- EXPLORATIONS, activities relating to the topic;
- EXPERIMENTS, usually associated with science topics;
- EXPEDITIONS, field trips;
- EXPLANATIONS, teacher helps or educational philosophies.

In the sidebars we also include Additional Layers, Famous Folks, Fabulous Facts, On the Web, and other extra related topics that can take you off on tangents, exploring the world and your interests with a bit more freedom. The curriculum will always be there to pull you back on track when you're ready.

You can learn more about how to use this curriculum at www.layers-of-learning.com/layers-of-learning-program/

BYZANTINES– TURKEY – CLIMATE & SEASONS – BYZANTINE ART

UNIT ONE
BYZANTINES – TURKEY – CLIMATE & SEASONS – BYZANTINE ART

The important thing is never to stop questioning.
-Albert Einstein

	LIBRARY LIST:
HISTORY	Search for: Byzantines, Byzantine Empire, Byzantium, Constantinople, Justinian ☺ ☺ ☺ Ancient Stories From The Dardanelles by Frances Delanoy Little. ☺ ☺ ☺ Constantinople: City on the Golden Horn from American Heritage Publishers. ☺ ☺ Byzantine Costumes Paper Dolls from Dover Publishers. ☺ Constantinople: The Forgotten Empire by Isaac Asimov. Out of print, look at your library or for used copies. ☺ The Byzantines by Thomas Caldecott Chubb. Out of print, look for used copies. ☺ Anna of Byzantium by Tracy Barrett. The story of a young princess of Byzantium and the intrigue that surrounded the royal court. ☺ The Emperor's Winding Sheet by Jill Patton Walsh. ☺ ☺ Byzantium: The Lost Empire from TLC (DVD). ☺ A Short History of Byzantium by John Julius Norwich. This book chronicles the history of Constantinople. ☺ Lost To The West by Lars Brownworth. Explains how the Byzantine Empire preserved civilization, literature, and science when the west fell. ☺ Road To Manzikert:Byzantine and Islamic Warfare by Brian Todd Carey. An illustrated parallel history of how the Byzantines and the Muslims made war. ☺ 1453: The Holy War For Constantinople and the Clash of Islam and the West by Roger Crowley. A well-written blow by blow account of the siege that destroyed Constantinople and led to the Ottoman Empire, told from both sides of the conflict. ☺ The Orphans of Byzantium by Timothy S. Miller.
GEOGRAPHY	Search for: Turkey, tales from Turkey, Istanbul ☺ ☺ ☺ Visit http://www.allaboutturkey.com/index.htm to find out lots about Turkey from its history to its culture. ☺ ☺ ☺ Folk Tales From Turkey by Serpil Ural. ☺ T Is for Turkey by Nilufer Topaloglu Pyper and Prodeepta Das. ☺ The Hungry Coat: A Tale From Turkey by Demi. ☺ A Donkey Reads by Muriel Mandell. ☺ Turkey by Madeline Donaldson. ☺ ☺ Turkish Delight: A Kids Guide To Turkey by Penelope Dyan. ☺ ☺ National Geographic Countries of the World: Turkey by Sarah Shields. ☺ Istanbul: The Imperial City by John Freely. A travel guide to the modern city of Istanbul, and a history guide to its rich past.

BYZANTINES – TURKEY – CLIMATE & SEASONS – BYZANTINE ART

SCIENCE

Search for: seasons, climate, micro-climate, winter, spring, summer, fall
- Seasons by Henry Pluckrose.
- Sunshine Makes the Seasons by Franklyn M. Branley.
- The Year at Maple Hill Farm by Alice Provensen.
- Bill Nye the Science Guy: Earth's Seasons DVD.
- Bill Nye the Science Guy: Climate DVD.
- Weather Watcher from DK. Full of information and activities you can use clear through the weather units. If there is one weather book to buy, this is it. (But see if the library has it first.)
- A Walk in the Desert by Rebecca L. Johnson: specific to North American climates.
- A Walk in the Boreal Forest by Rebecca L. Johnson: specific to North American climates.
- A Walk in the Prairie by Rebecca L. Johnson: specific to North American climates.
- A Walk in the Rain Forest by Rebecca L. Johnson: specific to North American climates.
- A Walk in the Tundra by Rebecca L. Johnson: specific to North American climates.
- Boom: The Weather and Climate Files From Discovery Channel Store.
- Frost Hollows and Other Microclimates by Lawrence P. Pringle.
- Arctic and Antarctic from DK Eyewitness.
- The Climate Crisis: An Introductory Guide To Climate Change by David Archer and Stefan Rahmstorf. Explains the science and the argument behind anthropomorphic climate change and the dangers it presents.
- Climate of Extremes: Global Warming Science They Don't Want You To Know About by Patrick J. Michaels and Robert Balling Jr. Takes the moderate position that anthropomorphic global warming is happening, but that there is no crisis looming.
- Climate: The Counter Consensus by Robert M. Carter. Makes the case that climate changes on the earth are natural and not man-made. Read all three books above and make up your own mind.

THE ARTS

Search for: Byzantine art
- The Art Museum from Phaidon Press. 1000 pages in a large format coffee table book of art from all over the world and from every era. It's expensive, but has all the images you'll ever need for a complete art history education. Check your library.
- Byzantine Art by Jannic Durand. Adult level text, but the images make this book for everyone, from your little ones on up.
- Treasury of Byzantine Ornament by Arne Dehli. Line drawings of 255 different architectural motifs used by the Byzantines and exported around the Mediterranean, especially Italy.
- Byzantine Art by Robin Cormack.
- Art of the Byzantine Era by David Talbot Rice.

BYZANTINES – TURKEY – CLIMATE & SEASONS – BYZANTINE ART

HISTORY: BYZANTINES

Fabulous Fact

This is a modern day satellite image of Istanbul showing the narrow strait, called the Bosporus, that leads into the Black Sea from the Sea of Marmara.

That narrow bit of sea plus the massive walls were the key to the defense of the city.

Fabulous Fact

The term "Byzantine" wasn't used until modern times. The people of that empire and their neighbors all called it "Rome."

But scholars wanted to separate it from the earlier Roman Empire. Do you think Byzantium is sufficiently different from the earlier Rome that it deserves a new name?

When the Roman Empire fell, it was really only the west that fell. Having grown so huge and unwieldy, the Empire had been split into two halves earlier. In the east, Roman life continued on as usual. The capital was at Byzantium, renamed Constantinople, and so the empire became known as the Byzantine Empire. It held steady and then grew under the emperor Justinian. Justinian and his wife, Empress Theodora, had a well run, organized Christian empire, powerful and dominant in the Mediterranean.

This is a mural of Constantinople showing the sea walls and the chains across the harbor, which defended the city.

The Byzantines were the bulwark against barbarians from the east and Arabs from the Middle East. Later, after the Muslim religion was founded and began to be spread by the sword, Byzantium became the shield wall defending Europe from the Muslims. But it wasn't only their enemies they had to contend with; the Empire (the city of Constantinople in particular) was rich with gold statuary, pottery, and precious stones.

In 1054 the Greek church split from Rome when disagreements over power and doctrine could not be resolved. The eastern church became the Greek Orthodox Church. And so the two Christian powers, who ought to have been allies, became rivals and sometimes enemies. The crusaders, who were supposedly coming to save Byzantium and Christianity in the

BYZANTINES – TURKEY – CLIMATE & SEASONS – BYZANTINE ART

Holy Land, could not resist, and on their way through to the Middle East they sacked the city of Constantinople. Later when the empire was facing its final destruction against the Muslims, no one from Europe would answer the call for help and the last of the Roman Empire finally fell in 1453, a thousand years after the fall of Rome.

🙂 🙂 🙂 EXPLORATION: Byzantine Timeline

There are printable timeline squares at the end of this unit. Place them on a wall timeline or in a book timeline.

- 330 AD Constantine makes Byzantium his capital and renames it Constantinople
- 527 AD Justinian becomes the emperor of the Eastern Roman Empire
- 639 AD Muslim armies conquer southern lands of the Empire: Syria, Holy Land, Egypt, Jordan
- 726 AD Emperor Leo III orders all icons (religious paintings) destroyed
- 843 AD Icons restored by Empress Theodora
- 1054 AD The Patriarch in Constantinople and the Pope in Rome excommunicate one another, splitting the church
- 1071 AD Seljuk Turks defeat Byzantines and take Asia Minor
- 1081 AD Byzantium defeats an attack from the Norman state of South Italy
- 1204 AD 4th Crusade; Crusaders occupy Constantinople and sack the city
- 1261 AD Constantinople is recaptured by Byzantine Emperor, Michael Palaeologus.
- 1300-1450 AD Byzantine Empire slowly loses land to the Turks until the city Constantinople stands alone
- 1453 AD Ottoman Turks take Constantinople.

Crusaders sacking the city of Constantinople in 1204 AD.

Additional Layer

This image is from an illuminated manuscript from the 12th century. The caption above the picture reads "the fleet of the Romans setting ablaze the fleet of the enemies." In this case the enemy was Slavic. Learn more about Greek fire.

Fabulous Fact

The use of standards and coats of arms was not a Greek one and the practice died out after the west fell. There was no official state emblem until the last couple of centuries of the empire when they adopted the old Hittite symbol of the double headed eagle.

BYZANTINES – TURKEY – CLIMATE & SEASONS – BYZANTINE ART

Famous Folks

Justinian is probably the most well known of the emperors of Byzantium. He expanded the empire until it was nearly as large as the previous Roman Empire. Read more about him and his fascinating wife, Theodora.

You can also color the portrait of Justinian from the end of this unit.

Writer's Workshop

Compare the emperors of the Byzantine Empire with our current political leaders. How do the forms of government differ? How did people gain power then? How do our leaders come to power now?

☺ ☺ ☺ **EXPLORATION: Byzantine Map**

The eastern Mediterranean fell after the Western Roman Empire. Use the Byzantine map from the end of this unit. Color the Byzantine lands red, the Ostrogoth Empire in blue, the Kingdom of Burgundy in purple, the Kingdom of Visigoths in green, the Kingdom of Vandals in orange, and the Kingdom of Franks in yellow. Some of the outlying empires and peoples are labeled on the map as well.

This map is only a snap shot in time of the years immediately after the fall of Rome. Later the Byzantine Empire will grow and shrink like a slinky, European kingdoms will disappear quicker than Houdini from a locked box, and a whole new empire, undreamed of at this time, and driven by a brand new religion of the Arabs, will rise up and threaten the entire world.

☺ **EXPLORATION: Constantine, A Christian**

When Constantine became the emperor, he felt he was sent by God to rule. He was a Christian, and he wanted all of his people to be Christian too. He told the Romans they had to become Christians.

Many times throughout history the leader of a nation determines the religion of his followers, either by official decree or just because they follow his example. Many countries have state religions and even state churches. A state religion is the adoption by the government of an official religion. A state church is

BYZANTINES – TURKEY – CLIMATE & SEASONS – BYZANTINE ART

different; it's when the government actually creates a church and has absolute control over it.

Do you think there should be a state church or a state religion? What are the pros and cons of religion mingled with government? What role do morals play in ruling and maintaining a nation? Write a persuasive essay outlining your reasons and beliefs for your point of view.

😊 🟢 EXPLORATION: Legal Name Change

Lots of people change their names for a variety of reasons. Cities change names too. Istanbul, the largest city in Turkey, has had its name changed lots of times. Its two most notable names were Byzantium, named after King Byzas, and Constantinople, in honor of Constantine the Great. He named it that himself. It's now known as Istanbul, which translated, means "the city."

Write a journal entry about names. Consider these questions:
- If you could change your name to anything, what would you call yourself? What meaning does it have?
- If you could change the name of your city/state to anything, what name would you choose? Why?
- If you were to found your very own brand new city, what would you name it?

😊 🟢 🔵 EXPLORATION: Justinian, Farmer Boy

Justinian was a boy who lived on a farm far away from Constantinople. He hated the idea of growing up to become a farmer. He begged to go to the city to live with his Uncle Justin and go to school. His parents said yes, and he moved to the city. He worked really hard in school and did well. After he was finished he joined the army. Eventually his Uncle Justin became the Emperor of the Byzantine Empire and Justinian helped him rule. By this time his uncle was getting old. He didn't have any children, and he loved Justinian like a son, so he adopted him. When his uncle died, Justinian became the emperor, a far cry from the farmer he first thought he might be!

What do you want to be when you grow up? Do you want to have the same job as someone else in your family? Decide on a career that you think might be fun, and then find out about it. How much schooling do you need? Will you need good grades? Where might you live? How much will you get paid? Talk to someone who has that job and ask them questions about what it's like.

Justinian also expanded the empire to its greatest extent, taking back many lands formerly held by Rome. Use the "Justinian's

---

Fabulous Fact

Byzantine emperors were considered chosen of God and the representative of Christ.

Starting with Diocletian, Constantine's predecessor, the Byzantine emperors discarded the old myth that they ruled a republic and openly declared themselves absolute autocratic rulers.

Additional Layer

Byzantium's great wealth came, you guessed it, from trade. The western end of the Silk Road lay in the Byzantine Empire and the most important port on the road was at a city called Trebizond, which lies on the southern coast of the Black Sea. From there, goods were taken to Byzantium, Greece, Italy, and Britain, mostly by Venetian and Genoese merchants who also became rich off the trade. At the end of the Byzantine Empire when they were besieged by the Ottoman Turks, the only ones to render any kind of aid were the Genoese who had commercial interests to protect.

How do commercial interests influence military and diplomatic actions by governments today? Should they?

BYZANTINES – TURKEY – CLIMATE & SEASONS – BYZANTINE ART

> **Additional Layer**
> Byzantine monasteries were the first in the world of their kind. Many such places established a thousand or more years ago are still functioning. They were the bastion of stability amid all the upheaval of the ages.

> **Additional Layer**
> Between 541 and 542 a horrible plague broke out in the eastern empire. Scholars estimate that as many as 40% of the population (around 25 million people total, or about 5,000 a day) died of the plague. The repercussions were enormous. Find out more.

> **Additional Layer**
>
> This is a miniature painting from the late Byzantine period depicting Alexander the Great who the Byzantines totally idolized as the greatest Greek ever.
>
> Is there a hero from history that you idolize? Why are they so great?

Empire" map from the end of this unit to color his empire. These lands won't be held for very long by the Byzantines. As the earlier Empire of Rome found, it is tough to keep so many different cultures and people united in one political entity.

Justinian's Empire 555 AD

😊 😊 EXPLORATION: Theodora

Theodora was Justinian's wife, and helped him rule the empire. Like Justinian, Theodora didn't have a royal background. In fact, her parents were circus performers at the Hippodrome. She herself was an actress there. She traveled all over the empire putting on shows. She was famous, but eventually she didn't want that life anymore. She became a spinner and made wool. No one knows how Justinian and Theodora met, but when they did, they fell in love. Theodora was in a lower social class and the two couldn't have been married except that Justinian, then a soldier, begged his emperor uncle to change the law. He did, and the two were married.

BYZANTINES – TURKEY – CLIMATE & SEASONS – BYZANTINE ART

Once when Constantinople was being attacked Justinian became afraid they would be killed. He wanted to run away from the city. Theodora said she would rather die than run away and she gave him the courage to stay. The armies were able to drive the invaders out and they were safe.

Are American first ladies (president's wives) involved in helping their husbands with their job as president? You can search at whitehouse.gov/about/first-ladies and read biographies about America's first ladies. Choose one of the first ladies to learn more about.

Is there a difference between a president's spouse and a king's consort? What are the differences? Why?

🙂 🟢 🟣 **EXPLORATION: The Code of Justinian**
Justinian made the empire much larger. He fixed it up and improved the buildings and roads. He had many beautiful churches built. He also made a set of laws called the Code of Justinian. They were strict, fair laws. They made sure that everyone lived by the same laws, whether rich or poor, male or female. Theodora helped make many of the laws, and she was one of the first rulers to consider women's rights.

Justinian didn't just make up random laws that he thought were best. He organized the laws already on the books and codified them so that they stood up in any court no matter where they were or who was involved. His law code had three parts initially.

The first was called the "codex" and included all imperial pronouncements made since the time of the emperor Hadrian. These were edited and organized and added to by Justinian's scholars.

The second part of the law code was called the "digesta" which included all judicial decisions made up to that point within the empire. It was edited down into a body of case law. We use case law in modern countries as well. Sometimes we call this "precedent." Today it has the force of tradition, but is not absolute. Precedents can be overturned. Justinian made the assembled and edited precedents absolute.

The third part of the code was called the "institutiones" and was a text book for law students. But it also had the complete force of absolute law and could be used in courts.

Later Justinian found it necessary to add to his law code where it

On The Web
Watch this four minute You Tube video of the differences between the Roman Empire and the Byzantine Empire:

http://youtu.be/FrAIPRNwpYo

Includes a map showing the changing borders.

Additional Layer
Justinian's laws influenced European laws through the Middle Ages, when it was simply called "Roman Law." Even today much of European law and international law in Europe comes straight out of Justinian's Codes. Other major law systems in the world today are English "common law" and "sharia" law.

Additional Layer
Justinian's law stated that you were only a citizen if you met certain conditions, among which was being a member of the Orthodox Church, which was the official state church.

Do you think there should be conditions for citizenship within the boundaries of a country? What should those conditions be and why?

What are the privileges of being a citizen?

BYZANTINES – TURKEY – CLIMATE & SEASONS – BYZANTINE ART

Additional Layer
Often cities are named after important people. Can you find some cities in your area that are named for people?

Additional Layer
They Might Be Giants sang a popular version of a song called 'Istanbul Not Constantinople." *The Four Lads* also performed a version of the song. You can see either version performed on You Tube.

Additional Layer
Irene of Athens became Empress of Byzantium in 797 when she began to rule in place of  her underage son, Constantine VI. When he grew up and wanted to rule she fought against him, eventually imprisoning him and having his eyes gouged out. The pope at Rome, seeing that the throne of the Roman Empire was vacant (a woman never ruled in Rome and didn't count) gave the title of Holy Roman Emperor to Charlemagne, king of the Franks.

was inadequate and this new addition was called the "novellae." Make a paper folding thing with the four parts of Justinian's law code on it. Here's how:

1. Start with a piece of computer paper and fold down one corner to make a triangle with even sides.

2. Cut off the flap of paper sticking out, so that you end up with a square piece of paper.

3. Open the paper and fold the other corner over so you have crease lines running across the center of the paper and corner to corner.

4. Fold each of the corners to the center.

5. Fold each of the corners to the center again.

6. Turn the paper over and fold the corners to the center one more time.

7. Open up the four flaps and insert your fingers into the "pockets".

8. Write "The Code Of Justinian" on the flaps, one word on each section. Lay the paper down flat to write and decorate.

9. Open the next layer and write "Novellae" "Codex" "Digesta" and "Institutiones" on each of the flaps.

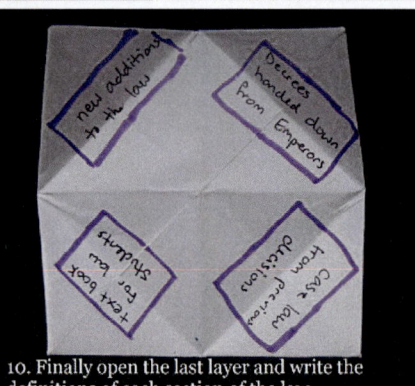
10. Finally open the last layer and write the definitions of each section of the law.

13

Byzantines – Turkey – Climate & Seasons – Byzantine Art

😊 🟢 EXPLORATION: Heraclius vs. Khosrau

Heraclius was the Byzantine emperor from 610 AD until 641 AD. He made Greek the official language of the empire, sent Christian missionaries to the people of the Balkans, and fought to protect his empire from first the Persians, and then the militant new Arab religion called Islam, becoming the first Christian monarch to come up against the Muslims. His greatest foe though was Khosrau, the king of Persia.

Khosrau submitting before Heraclius, from an enamel plaque (c. 116-1170AD).

Several years before Heraclius came to the throne the current Byzantine emperor, Maurice, had helped Khosrau, the emperor of Persia to regain his throne, so Khosrau felt loyal to Maurice. But an upstart Byzantine usurper named Phocas, who has always been remembered as a bitter tyrant, had Maurice and his entire family killed, stealing the throne for himself. Khosrau was enraged and prepared for battle, rapidly retaking the Byzantine province of Mesopotamia which had formerly belonged to Persia. Phocas, being the tyrant he was, didn't have long before another general took power. This one was named Heraclius and his son, who was also named Heraclius, was given the throne. By now it was the year 611 and the Persians had taken Syria and were marching through Anatolia, virtually unopposed since the Byzantines had been too busy fighting over the succession to watch their own borders.

Heraclius returning the True Cross to Jerusalem in this painting by Miguel Jiménez y Martín Bernat (1481)

In 613 Heraclius finally fought back and was soundly defeated at Antioch. The way was now clear for the Persians to march to

Additional Layer

Heraclius had a dream that an army of "The Circumcised Man" would be victorious against all his enemies. At first Heraclius thought this meant the Jews, but later he heard of a new leader, a man who had managed to unite the Arab tribes, a thing which never had been done before. The man was named Mohammad and his followers called him a prophet.

Additional Layer

Piero della Francesca painted a series of frescos in the city of Arezzo, Italy in the early Renaissance period called "The History of the True Cross." His finest painting is of Heraclius vs. Khosrau and the regaining of the cross which had been stolen.

Detail from the painting by Piero

Byzantines – Turkey – Climate & Seasons – Byzantine Art

Women

Women could own property, inherit and pass down property, own and run businesses, receive protection of the law equally with men, and maintain control over their own dowries. Culturally, women were the heads of their households while men participated in public life. Boys were usually better educated than girls as well.

Famous Folks

It was Patriarch Sergius of the Church who convinced Heraclius not to abandon the city of Constantinople to Khosrau. Patriarch Sergius had acted as regent while Heraclius was away fighting battles. Sergius had to defend the city against an invading army of Slavs, but before going to battle he led a litany in the church and immediately a storm swept in and destroyed the enemy army. All hailed it as a miracle.

Additional Layer

By the time of Heraclius' death an Arab named Muhammad would lead armies that would take the Levant again and also Egypt.

Constantinople, which they did, camping across the Bosporus. By 621 the Persians had taken Palestine and Egypt as well. While they were in Jerusalem the Persians went and stole the most holy relic in the Christian world from the Church of the Holy Sepulcher, the "True Cross" upon which Christ was hung.

Meanwhile in the north, the Slavs and the Avars knew an opportunity when they saw one and took over large sections of the Balkans. Heraclius had lost nearly the entire empire in just twenty years. Not much more than the city of Constantinople stood. He did still hold a section of the northern coast of Africa and Heraclius thought of abandoning Constantinople and fleeing to Carthage, but in the end he decided to make a fight of it.

First, Heraclius bought himself some time by agreeing to pay a tribute of 1000 talents of gold, 1000 talents of silver, 1000 silk robes, 1000 horses, and 1000 virgins to the Persian Khosrau in exchange for peace. Having paid up, Heraclius immediately began preparing for war by slashing spending, restructuring the currency, melting down church relics and ornaments to raise cash, and giving the army a new purpose by making it all into a Holy War, carrying icons of Christ before them as battle standards.

In 622 Heraclius was marching across Asia Minor defeating everyone who came in his way. Then he marched north and took on the Slavs in the Balkans. In 627 he beat the Persians soundly at Nineveh and marched south and sacked Khosrau's palace, retaking that piece of the Holy Cross. Khosrau was killed by his own people for his failures and his son sued for peace. Heraclius, with much pomp and splendor, carried the Holy Cross back to the city of Jerusalem and the Empire was saved for another generation.

Persia never recovered from this defeat and they were slowly absorbed and conquered by the new Muslim state.

Play the "Treasure of the Cross" game from the end of this unit. Directions on how to play are printed on the game board. Besides the game board you'll need colored "men' to place on your cities (colored rocks, beads, pencil erasers, or Legos work well), six of each color, and four dice.

☺ ☻ EXPLORATION: Byzantine Dress-Up

Make some Byzantine clothes. Start with a long under-dress, like a big t-shirt that hangs near your ankles. It's called a tunica. Men and women wore this first layer. Wealthy people wore more

Byzantines – Turkey – Climate & Seasons – Byzantine Art

layers of clothing over the tunica, but the peasants only got that. It was usually plain, but for the wealthy the tunica would have been made using fine materials like silk.

Next you need an overdress; again, both men and women wore these. They were called dalmatica. Use an old sheet or curtain fabric to make a triangular shaped garment, flaring as it nears the ground, with long triangular or bell shaped sleeves. Bright colors were worn, but the Emperor and Empress were the only ones who were allowed to wear purple. The Byzantines were wealthy in general and their clothes had jewels, fancy trim and embroideries. You can add rick rack, lace trim, and glass or plastic "jewels" to your clothes to make them fancy.

This is an emperor and empress of Byzantium. They wear cloaks and crowns over their tunica and dalmatica.

Additional Layer

Byzantine writers wrote religious tracts and sermons, adventure and romance stories, histories, and chronicles. Chronicles are like histories except for a popular audience. Histories were very scholarly.

Additional Layer

In spite of the powerful cities sprinkled around the empire, most people were farmers and lived in small villages in the countryside. They farmed vineyards, vegetable gardens, olive groves, and wheat and barley fields, and raised cattle and sheep. Their homes were a couple of rooms with a packed dirt floor and thatched roofs for the poorest and timber framed houses with two stories for the more well-to-do. Every farmer had to sell some of his produce for money if only to pay the taxes.

The village peasants owned their own land. Then there were those who labored on the large estates of the wealthy. The estate farmers did not own land and did not pay taxes, but never fear, the estate owners got it out of them. By the end of the Empire most of the land was held by estates.

BYZANTINES – TURKEY – CLIMATE & SEASONS – BYZANTINE ART

Famous Folks

Princess Anna Comnena was a scholar, hospital director, doctor, and history writer, having written *Alexiad*, an account of her father's reign. She was highly educated in all the learning of her day. But she had to sneak off and read the Iliad in secret because her parents thought it too pagan and too violent.

Additional Layer

GDP stands for Gross Domestic Product and means "how much is all the stuff you produce as a nation worth?"

In 1990 dollars the estimated GDP of the Byzantine Empire was about $13 billion. Modern day Turkey's GDP in 1990 dollars was about $150 billion. The United States' GDP was approximately $5 trillion in 1990.

But the population of a country greatly affects the number. Byzantium had perhaps 18 million people. Modern Turkey has 73 million and the U.S. has some 300 million. So a better number to compare is the GDP per capita. Can you figure it out?

☺ ☺ ☺ EXPLORATION: Constantinople

We learned that Rome fell, but in a way, only part of it did. Since the empire had been divided into eastern and western regions, it was only the west that fell. Constantinople was the capital city for the eastern part, the Byzantine Empire. In a lot of ways Constantinople was similar to Rome. It was built on seven hills just like Rome and it was surrounded by a wall just like Rome.

Byzantine emperors also ruled much more like Romans than like the Barbarian tribes surrounding them. They made sure that the poor had access to cheap grain and provided security for the city. There were big differences though. The Byzantines were an eclectic mix of peoples – Greeks, Jews, Romans, Egyptians, Christians, and Goths. They had different religious beliefs, spoke different languages, and came from lots of areas of the world. Rome consisted of Romans who all spoke Latin and worshiped Roman gods.

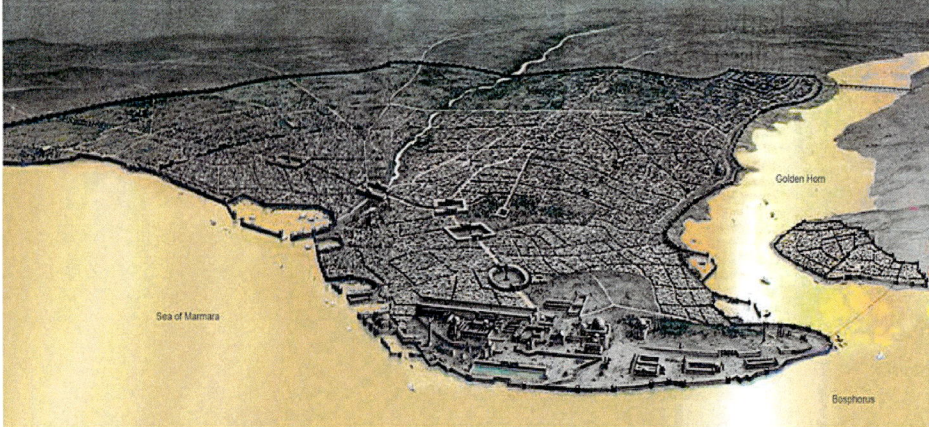

This is the ancient City of Constantinople sitting on a peninsula of land that juts out just at the western end of the Bosporus Strait.

Divide a sheet of paper in half. On one side, write "Rome" and on the other write "Constantinople." List the characteristics you know about each city. Are there some things common to both lists? How are they different?

Or Do a Venn Diagram:
Draw 2 overlapping circles to create a Venn Diagram. Label one "Romans" and the other "Byzantines." Write these facts in the appropriate places:

Romans:	Byzantines:	Both:
Believed in many gods	Believed in one God	Were all part of the Roman Empire originally
Spoke Latin primarily	Spoke mostly Greek	Called themselves Romans
Empire fell in 476 AD	Survived the fall of Rome	
In the west	In the east	

Byzantines – Turkey – Climate & Seasons – Byzantine Art

☺ ☺ ☻ **EXPEDITION: Hippodrome**
Like their Roman neighbors, the Byzantines loved to be entertained. They had a Hippodrome, similar to the Roman Circus Maximus, where they went to watch shows. There were circus acts, chariot races, and performances galore. It could hold about 100,000 spectators.

The Hippodrome is in ruins today, but you can use your computer to go on a virtual tour of what it looked like. Byzantium 1200 is a website devoted to re-creating images of what Byzantium (also called Constantinople) would have looked like in the Middle Ages. Visit www.Byzantium1200.com; from their website, click on "Hippodrome" in the sidebar menu. You'll see amazing images of the stadium, complete with the horseshoe-shaped racetrack.

☺ ☻ **EXPLORATION: Greed**
A wise person once said, "Hide Your Money." Byzantium's wealth eventually became a big lure for a crusading army from Egypt. Not only did the soldiers attack the city for its wealth, they also destroyed huge amounts of art, literature, and holy relics. The attackers chalked it up to teaching those Greeks a lesson. Constantinople couldn't recover from such huge losses, and was then unable to counter the threat from the Ottoman Turks. An Ottoman army of over 80,000 men attacked the city and the Byzantine Empire fell.

Play a game called "Hide The Coins." Hide 10 coins in a pre-specified room. Have all the kids search for the coins. For each coin found, have the students tell you a way that people can hide their wealth. Why is it safer for a person to hide their wealth? Is it possible for a city or country to "hide" its wealth?

☺ ☺ ☻ **EXPLORATION: The Legend of Constantine Palaiologos**
There is a legend that the last Emperor of Byzantium, Constantine XI, whose body was never found after the walls were taken, was carried away by an angel, hidden in a cave, and will remain frozen in time until the Christian Empire is restored and he will reign again.

Write your own version of the legend in your Writer's Notebook.

Additional Layer

Look at the southern border of modern day Turkey. That border is the line the Byzantine emperors held against the encroaching Muslim armies until the Ottoman Turks finally took the Empire.

On the Web

Watch this You Tube video, http://youtu.be/DjmZgtHt8y4

An illustrated timeline, set to music, of some of the most pivotal events in the Byzantine history.

Additional Layer

The Byzantine Empire fell to the Ottomans in 1453 AD. Businessmen, scholars, artists, and merchants fled to Italy where they already had ties with the Venetians and Genoese. When they fled, they brought with them ancient Greek and Roman manuscripts. The Italian Renaissance took off starting in the mid-1400's. Coincidence? I don't think so.

BYZANTINES – TURKEY – CLIMATE & SEASONS – BYZANTINE ART

GEOGRAPHY: TURKEY

Teaching Tip
As you learn about a country in the world, first find it on a map or preferably a globe of the earth. Point it out to your kids and identify its continent. How far from your home town is it?

Writer's Workshop
Create a photo essay or slideshow presentation about Turkey. Include subsections about food, holidays, geography, economy, general life, and other interesting topics.

Additional Layer
Mt. Ararat is the highest peak in Turkey. It is also the mountain that many people believe Noah's Ark came to rest on.

Additional Layer
Approximately 98% of the population of Turkey is Muslim, but few women wear a face veil, they do not use sharia law, and church and state are completely separated. It is a western country with an Islamic faith. Learn more about Islam.

The modern state of Turkey was born out of the remnants of the Ottoman Empire, the people who had defeated the Byzantines. It lies in Asia Minor and across the Bosporus to the southeastern tip of Europe. The capital is Istanbul, formerly known as Constantinople.

Turkey is a democratic republic, with a civil government, not a religious one. It has a constitution and a parliament. Its governmental form is based on European governments. The country is almost all Muslim.

Istanbul with the Marmara Sea in the background. Photo from Istanbul and Türkei Community and shared under CC license.

😀 😊 🙂 **EXPLORATION: Map of Turkey**
Use the map of Turkey from the end of this unit and a student atlas or a guide book of Turkey to find and label the following locations:

Label these cities:
- Istanbul
- Ankara
- Izmir
- Bursa
- Konya
- Trabzon

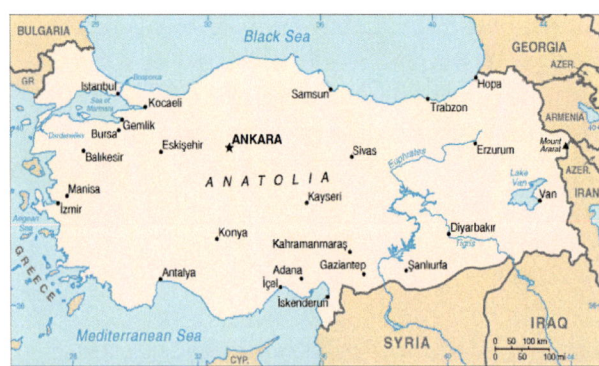

BYZANTINES – TURKEY – CLIMATE & SEASONS – BYZANTINE ART

- Adana
- Samsun

Color each of these regions in a different color:
- Aegean
- Marmara
- Central Anatolia
- Mediterranean
- Southeast Anatolia
- Eastern Anatolia
- Black Sea

Label and color the seas and lakes of Turkey.
- Mediterranean Sea
- Sea of Marmara
- Black Sea
- Bosporus
- Lake Tuz
- Lake Van (a shallow salt lake)

Now glue your map onto a large poster-board. Print or draw pictures of features from each of the regions of Turkey around your map. Draw a line from each picture to its location on your map. Some things you might want to include:

- Mt. Ararat
- City of Troy
- Taurus Mountains
- Cappadocia, fairy chimneys
- Cappadocia, underground cities
- Calcium deposits of Pamukkale
- Grand Bizarre of Istanbul
- Hagia Sofia
- Pergamum Ruins
- Use a guide book of Turkey for more

😊 ☺ EXPLORATION: Sports

People in Turkey do many of the same sports you do – skiing, swimming, golf, hunting, fishing, rafting, and more. Turkey's most popular sport is one you know all about, football. No, not American football; you would call it soccer. It's the most popular sport in the world and one of the first truly international sports.

One sport that is purely Turkish is Camel Wrestling. Two male camels butt at each other and use their necks to twist each other

---

Additional Layer

Turkey's education system is very similar to that of the U.S. because the same man, John Dewey, designed both. The American Dewey was invited over by Ataturk to help make education reforms in the country.

Famous Folks

Orhan Pamuk is a Turkish born, Nobel prize winning, best selling, assassin targeted, outspoken, government defying writer. His not keeping quiet about political sins in Turkey has had serious consequences to this Columbia University professor. His biggest faux pas? Supporting equal political rights for the Kurdish minority in Turkey. Find out more about him.

BYZANTINES – TURKEY – CLIMATE & SEASONS – BYZANTINE ART

Fabulous Fact
Turkey is famous for its woven rugs. They are most often made expertly of wool by hand.

Photo by Randy Oostdyk and shared under CC license.

On The Web
http://www.nashjaffer.net/ist3_rumeli_fortress.htm

Visit this site to learn more about the Rumeli Fortress.

Additional Layer

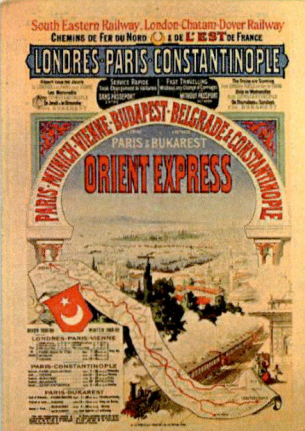

The Orient Express was an international Railway Line that ran from Paris to Istanbul. It was always viewed as a luxurious and exotic way to travel and Istanbul as a luxurious and exotic place to travel to. Learn more about this historic railway line.

to the ground until one is vanquished and charges toward the crowd who must scramble out of its way. Bets are made on which camel will win. The camels are often named after politicians and world leaders. They are also draped with fancy colorful rugs, and camel beauty contests are often a part of the festivities.

Make a standing camel craft using the craft sheet from the end of this unit. Color the camel, then cut it out, leaving the line in the middle uncut. Fold along the line and then stand your camel up.

Read an account of a spectators experience at a camel wrestling event here: http://www.turkeysforlife.com/2011/02/camel-wrestling-fethiye-turkey.html

😊 😊 😊 **EXPLORATION: Turkish Feast**
Make ajvar, a dip for pita bread or veggies

Peel and cut up 1 eggplant.
Boil in water until tender.
Blend in a food processor until smooth.

Add:
- 3 red sweet peppers, diced
- salt and pepper to taste
- 1 t. garlic powder
- 1/8 c. lemon juice
- ¼ cup olive oil

Mix all the ingredients in.

<u>Kebabs</u>: Skewering and grilling meat and veggies on a stick

Byzantines – Turkey – Climate & Seasons – Byzantine Art

originated in the Turkish area. Cube meat (lamb, beef, chicken) and vegetables and thread them onto a shish kabob stick (you can buy them in the grocery store).

Some Turkish vegetables include:
    eggplant
    zucchini
    tomatoes
    green peppers
    onions

Grill the kabobs outdoors over charcoal or a gas grill. You can also bake them in an oven at 350 degrees for about 30 minutes.

Serve over rice or with pita bread.

☺ ☺ ☺ **EXPLORATION: Turkish Treats**
The Turkish people are very fond of combinations of fruit and nuts. Their children eat fruit and nuts the way American children eat candy, as a special treat.

One famous Turkish treat is called Kuru Incir Tatlisi, or poached, stuffed figs.

    8-10 dried figs, stems removed
    ½ cup finely chopped walnuts
    ¼ cup sugar
    1 tsp. lemon juice

Famous Folks

Mustafa Kemal Ataturk led the resistance movement against the allies following WWI. The Ottoman Empire had fallen and there was a government vacuum into which France and England wished to step.

Ataturk was successful and became the first president of his country.

The name "Ataturk" means father of the Turks and was granted to Mustafa as a surname by the parliament. His influence on Turkey cannot be overstated. Read more about him.

Additional Layer

Learn more about flags, their history and anatomy. Read *Flag* by William Crampton, an Eyewitness book from DK.

BYZANTINES – TURKEY – CLIMATE & SEASONS – BYZANTINE ART

Additional Layer
Turkey is the largest producer of hazelnuts in the world. They grow along the coast of the Black Sea.

Additional Layer
Some Nasreddin Hodja tales appear in other places. Many countries claim the fictional author as their own, and his name has many spellings depending on where you are. Some of his stories even appear in Aesop's Fables. With stories this old, especially those passed down through oral tradition, it's very hard to know the exact origins.

Additional Layer

Lake Van is a salt lake, having no outlet to the sea. In 1995 the Lake Van monster, a plesiosaur-looking creature, was first sighted.

Poach the figs in enough simmering water to cover for 30 minutes. Remove the figs, reserving the cooking liquid. Cut a slit in the figs and stuff with the chopped walnuts. Meanwhile, dissolve the sugar in the water and boil for 2 minutes. Remove from the heat and stir in the lemon juice. Pour the syrup over the figs and serve warm.

EXPLORATION: Color a Turkish flag.
The flag of Turkey is red with a white crescent moon and a white star.

The red symbolizes the blood of the soldiers who fought in the war for independence of 1919 to 1923. The white star and moon represent independence. The crescent moon and star are Islamic symbols, but their use in Turkey goes back further than Islam. The crescent moon is a symbol of the Greek Goddess Diana and the star represented the Virgin Mary. There are other legends surrounding the symbolism of this flag that are worthwhile to read about.

😊 😊 😊 **EXPLORATION: The Tales of Nasreddin Hodja**
Nasreddin Hodja is Turkey's trickster. It's said he was born in 1208 in Horto, a small Turkish village. About 350 stories have been attributed to him, all with a good degree of wit in them. The word "hodja" means "teacher." In each tale, Nasreddin was trying to teach us something, so as you read his tales, look for the moral in the story.

Nasreddin figure from a theme park in Ankara. Photo by Nevit Dilman and shared under CC license.

BYZANTINES – TURKEY – CLIMATE & SEASONS – BYZANTINE ART

You can search for Nasreddin Hodja stories online and read many of them. Here is a short one to get you started. While you're reading, have the kids illustrate the tale and then write the moral below.

<u>Everyone is Right</u>
Once when Nasreddin Hodja was serving as qadi, one of his neighbors came to him with a complaint against another neighbor. The Hodja listened very carefully and then concluded, "Yes, dear neighbor, you are quite right."

Soon the other neighbor came to him. Again, the Hodja took time to listen carefully to his side of the story. He concluded, "Yes, dear neighbor, you are quite right."

The Hodja's wife heard all this and came to him. She said, "Husband, both men cannot be right."

The Hodja answered, "Yes, dear wife, you are quite right."

😊 😊 😊 EXPLORATION: Whirling Dervishes
The members of the Mevlevi Order, known in the west as Whirling Dervishes, live in Mevlevihane (what we would call monasteries). The religious sect was founded in Turkey and is known for the ceremony of the whirling dances they do. This ritual whirling is an expression of love and faith. It is supposed to have a mesmerizing effect that can induce a feeling of soaring and ecstasy.

Search on You Tube for "Whirling Dervishes" to watch examples of their dances and hear the music they dance to. You can twirl along to the music if you'd like to.

😊 EXPLORATION: Black Cats and Voodoo Dolls
Many places around the world have unique superstitions, and Turkey is no exception. Here are just a few Turkish superstitions:
- If a child constantly cries, someone in that house will die.
- If a shoe turns upside down when being taken off, it is believed that the owner of the shoe will die in the near future.
- It's bad luck to break a mirror.
- It's forbidden to sleep in a graveyard.
- A snake in a house guards it.
- When a wolf howls, the weather will be cold and snowy.
- A black cat crossing in front of a person is bad luck.
- Cracking your knuckles is a sign of good health.

Additional Layer
Turkey gets a lot of earthquakes. Learn more about earthquakes and what causes them. Why are there a lot of earthquakes in Turkey?

On the Web
Visit http://kids.nationalgeographic.com/kids/places/find/turkey/

to learn more about Turkey, geared just for kids from National Geographic.

Fabulous Fact

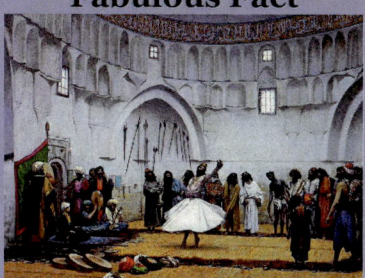

Dervishes began whirling when one wanted to commune with God after his good friend died. Out in the street, he was entranced by the rhythmic sound of a goldsmith's hammer and began to whirl (or twirl). He kept time with the hammer and began this fast rhythmic dance to become closer to God. They say you can enter a religious trance from the special dance.

Byzantines – Turkey – Climate & Seasons – Byzantine Art

Writer's Workshop

Write a story called "Superstitious." Follow a character throughout one day in which all kinds of superstitious events happen (crossing a black cat's path, for example.) Now YOU decide the outcome. Do all of those events mean doom? Does your character find a lucky way to ward off the superstitions? Or does your character find they have no merit at all?

Additional Layer

The Hagia Sofia was built as a Christian church by the Byzantines. The Turkish Muslims turned it into a mosque after they took Constantinople. Today it is a museum.

Learn more about the Hagia Sofia online.

Photo by Dennis Jarvis, CC license

- Anyone who has a foot itch will get to go on holiday.

Did you spot any superstitions you've heard before? Write down or tell about some superstitions you know about or believe in.

😊 EXPLORATION: Animals

Van cats, Persian cats, angora rabbits, Denizli roosters, and Kangal dogs were all bred in Turkey. You can learn more about these animals online.

The bald ibis is a rare type of bird that is native to Turkey, southern Europe, North Africa, and the surrounding areas. It is extinct in the wild in most of these areas. There is now a breeding program underway to save the animals. Turkey now has a semi-wild population.

Make a bald ibis headband hat. You need construction paper in black and orange, glue and scissors.

Attach skinny paper strips of black to the back of and sticking up from a black headband. Attach an orange triangular bill.

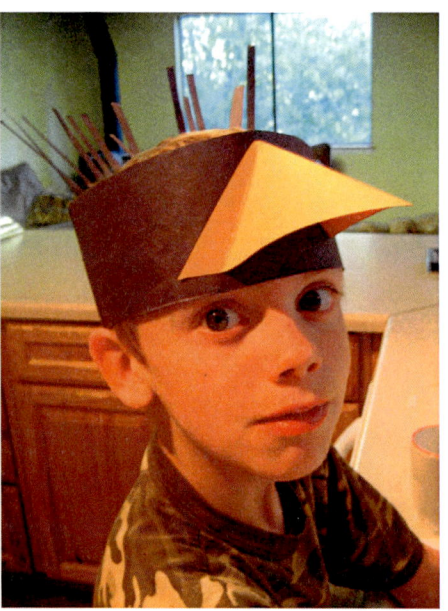

Choose one of the Turkish-bred species to learn more about, then make a project that reflects something you found out about your animal.

Science: Climate & Seasons

The earth turns on its axis and sometimes faces toward the sun and sometimes away; that's why we have days and nights. But because the earth is tilted, we also have seasons. When the northern hemisphere is tilted toward the sun, it is summer in the north, since the north is a bit closer to the sun and therefore, warmer. When it is tilted away it is winter, because it is a bit further from the sun, and therefore, colder. How big an effect does the sun have on our earth?

Climates are large areas that have similar weather. In the far north it is cold and frozen year round. This is an arctic climate. Near the equator it is hot and sunny all year; this is a tropical climate. Climate depends on latitude, how far away from the equator a place is, and also altitude, how high in elevation it is. The distance from the sea and ocean currents also have a big effect on climate. England, with warm ocean currents is much warmer than Newfoundland, Canada, which is about the same latitude.

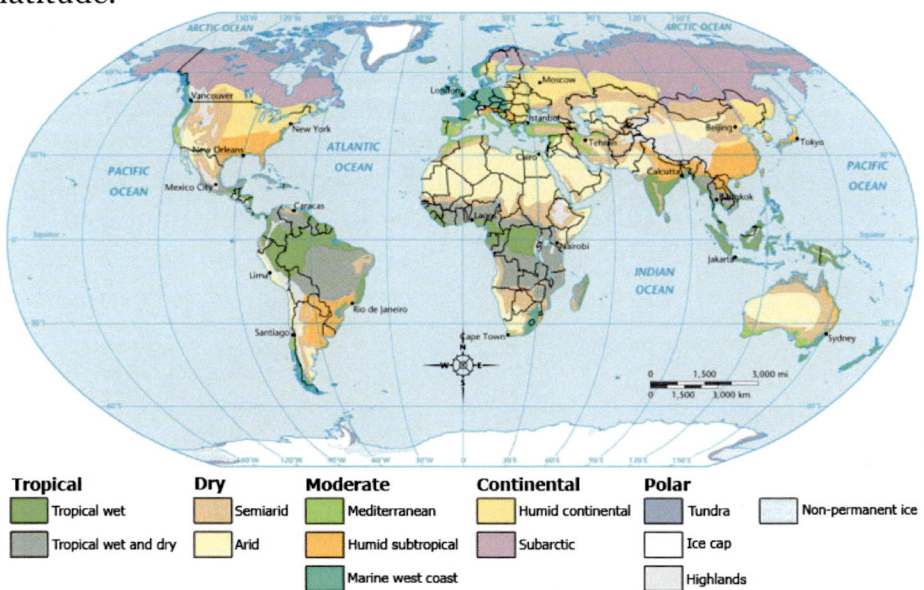

There are also micro-climates. Areas within a particular climate area that are slightly warmer or cooler than the surrounding area. Cities create micro-climates that are warmer because of all the concrete and asphalt. Bodies of water also create micro-climates that are warmer and wetter than the surrounding climate.

Climates on earth cycle naturally through warmer and cooler periods. That is why fossils of tropical plants have been

> **Additional Layer**
>
> Research possible ways humans might affect climate. And check into greenhouse gases. What are they, where do they come from, what do they do?

> **Additional Layer**
>
>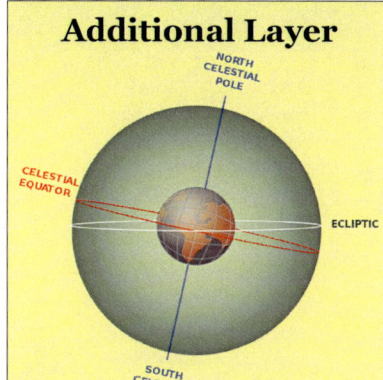
>
> Why is Earth's axis tilted? No one really knows for sure. We wonder if maybe it was struck by a large planet long, long ago.

> **Additional Layer**
>
> At the north and south poles summer means 24 hours of light and winter means 24 hours of darkness.
>
> Can you demonstrate this using a globe and a flashlight?

> **Writer's Workshop**
>
> Write an acrostic poem about each of the seasons.

Byzantines – Turkey – Climate & Seasons – Byzantine Art

Fabulous Facts

The tilt of the earth means that different hemispheres experience opposite seasons. When it is summer in the northern hemisphere, it's winter in the southern.

Some areas have regularly recurring weather events, and we refer to those as seasons too. Hurricane season and wildfire season are common in different areas of the United States.

Tropical regions don't experience four seasons. Instead, they usually have a wet season and a dry season.

Weather Lore

Groundhog's Day is a popular tradition in America. We all watch to see if the groundhog sees his shadow (if it's sunny enough for a shadow to form) on February 2nd. If so, we'll have 30 more days of winter weather. If not, spring has arrived.

Fabulous Fact

The hottest day of the year happens about a month after the earth is tilted closest to the sun. The gases in the atmosphere take awhile to absorb the heat, so there's a seasonal lag.

---

found in northern places. We also know the earth has been much colder in the past, as in the Ice Age. Scientists don't completely understand why the earth goes through these cycles, but it is probably related to the heat of the sun and the nearness of the sun to the earth, since the sun determines all weather patterns on Earth.

☺ **EXPLORATION: 4 Seasons**

Divide a poster board into four equal quadrants. Using magazines, cut out pictures of each of the seasons to paste into the quadrants. If you live in a place other than a temperate four season climate, you may want to adjust the project to your area.

☺ ☻ **EXPERIMENT: Heat**

All the weather on Earth is caused by the sun's heat. The heat affects temperature, but also air movement. Heat keeps air in motion, causing wind. Heat also evaporates water more quickly, creating rain and snow.

You'll need: water, a pot, a stove, a balloon, and a canning jar with a narrow top.

1. Boil some water in a pot on the stove. You'll need about 2 inches in the bottom of the pot.
2. Stretch the balloon over the mouth of the jar.
3. Take the pan off the stove and then place the jar with the balloon into the water. Watch it for a few minutes and observe what happens.

27

Byzantines – Turkey – Climate & Seasons – Byzantine Art

You can see the balloon blowing up as the warm air molecules are moving around inside of it. As the sun heats our earth up, it also causes warm air to move. That's why we have wind.

😊 ☺ EXPLORATION: Days and Seasons
Use a globe and a flashlight in a dim room to show how the earth's rotation makes day on one side while it's night on the other. Also use this method to show how the earth's tilt makes seasons happen as the earth moves around the sun. Use at least two helpers and design a demonstration of this.

☺ EXPLORATION: Four Seasons at My House
Draw a picture of your house in each season. If you live in a warmer climate you can show the seasons you have, wet and dry for example.

☺ EXPLORATION: Four Season Tree
Divide a piece of paper into four parts. In each part draw a tree trunk. Set out finger paints and dab on finger painted leaves in each color.

☺ EXPLORATION: Hand Trees
This is another variation of the four season tree. Trace your hand 4 times on sheets of brown construction paper. Cut them out and glue each one to a piece of light blue construction paper. Using tissue squares, glue the tissue paper to each tree, making it look

Explanation
Dinner Science Theater is becoming a favorite event at our place. Dad, our resident science-enthusiast, is our regular presenter. We sit at the family dinner table while Dad entertains us with cool science facts, discussions, and demonstrations.

Oh look, Dad made a cloud in the freezer!

Dinner Science Theater isn't planned. It isn't formal. We don't schedule it. What makes it fun is that you never know just when Dad might jump out of his seat and put on an amazing science show.

I guess one of the things I love best about homeschooling is that our learning doesn't stop just because it's 3:30. A science lesson over dinner is often even better remembered than one during "school time."

Byzantines – Turkey – Climate & Seasons – Byzantine Art

Writer's Workshop

Seasons and Senses Poems:

Choose a season and then write how it affects your senses.

Spring looks like . . .
Spring sounds like . . .
Spring feels like . . .
Spring smells like . . .
Spring tastes like . . .

Additional Layer

The ancient Greeks believed that the goddess Persephone was to blame for the changing of the seasons. She was the daughter of Zeus and Demeter, the harvest goddess. Greeks thought the fields grew dormant and lifeless for awhile because Demeter was unhappy about Persephone marrying Hades, the god of the underworld.

Persephone returning to Earth and bringing the spring. Painting by Frederick Leighton (1891)

like the leaves of each season. This is easy if you wrap each square around the eraser of your pencil, dab it in glue, then stick it down. Winter will have white tissue for snow. Fall will have yellow, orange, brown, and red. Spring will have light green. Summer will have dark green. You may want to make this into a booklet.

☺ ☺ **EXPLORATION: Animals**

Seasonal change doesn't just affect plants and people. A lot of animals are affected too. In the winter there's less available food and less warmth. Discuss some animals that change their lifestyles depending upon the season. Here are a few to get you started:

- bears
- butterflies
- birds
- deer
- geese
- honeybees
- squirrels
- manatees

☺ ☺ **EXPLORATION: Nature's Timekeepers**

We use the sun and moon to tell time. Why is a day 24 hours? Why is a year 365 days long? Demonstrate this (or have your student demonstrate it) with a globe and a flashlight. The globe will spin and also orbit around the sun (the flashlight).

Byzantines – Turkey – Climate & Seasons – Byzantine Art

☺ ☺ ☺ **EXPLORATION: Sundial**

Make a sundial and put it in the yard. It can be as simple as a stick stuck in a paper plate and set out in the yard, or much more complex and permanent. You can draw marks on each hour to show where the shadow is, and at the end of the day you'll have a fairly accurate timekeeping device.

Writer's Workshop

Hellos and Goodbyes Through the Year Poem

Fill in the blanks in this poem:

It is spring.
Hello _____.
Goodbye _____.
It is summer.
Hello _____.
Goodbye_____.
It is autumn.
Hello_____.
Goodbye _____.
It is winter.
Hello _____.
Goodbye_____.

Famous Folks

Astronomer Edward Maunder married Annie Russell who had been his assistant, and together they studied the sun and sun spots. Studying the record, they found that there had been no sun spots from 1645 to 1715. During this same time the earth cooled enough for the Thames River in England to freeze over in a time known as the "Little Ice Age."

The Frozen Thames by Abraham Hopndius (1677).

The Maunders concluded there must be a connection. What do you think?

BYZANTINES – TURKEY – CLIMATE & SEASONS – BYZANTINE ART

Famous Folks

Learn more about James Croll, the guy who first figured out that the change of the tilt of the earth on its axis was the cause of cyclical climate changes on Earth, as in from a warmer Earth to an ice age.

Additional Layer

Learn some weather folklore sayings. Here are a couple to get you started:

A sunshiny shower won't last half an hour.

Red at night, sailors' delight; red in the morning, sailors' warning.

Clear moon, frost soon.

Rain by seven, gone by eleven.

The higher the clouds, the better the weather.

A year of snow is a year of plenty.

☺ ☺ ☺ **EXPLORATION: Ice Age**
On a world map, show the extent of the ice during the last Ice Age and the extent of the ice now. Use the map from the end of this unit.

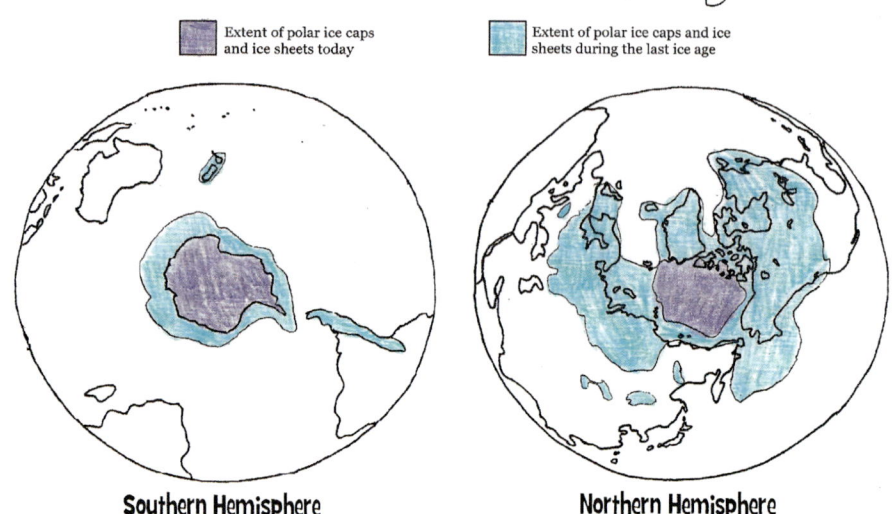

☺ ☺ ☺ **EXPLORATION: Weather Log**
During this, and all units that have to do with weather, you should keep a weather log. Spend some time outside making observations, taking measurements, and recording your findings. Track the temperature, clouds, and conditions. You can make this log a daily part of your morning routine so that when you study weather you'll have your own log to reference.

☺ ☺ **EXPERIMENT: The Greenhouse Effect**
The greenhouse effect means that heat from the sun gets trapped here on Earth, making the earth warmer than it would otherwise be. The greenhouse effect is natural and is caused by greenhouse gases. Greenhouse gases include water vapor, carbon dioxide, carbon monoxide, CFC's, and other minor gases. All of these except for CFC's exist in the atmosphere naturally. Humans contribute somewhat to the amount of carbon dioxide and carbon monoxide, but have no effect on water vapor.

To show how the greenhouse effect works you need two jars, some water, ice cubes, a plastic bag, and a thermometer.

1. Put two cups of cold water into each jar.
2. Add five ice cubes to each jar.
3. Cover one jar with a plastic bag (it doesn't need to be tight)
4. Leave both jars in the sun for one hour.
5. Check the temperatures of each jar.

Byzantines – Turkey – Climate & Seasons – Byzantine Art

The jar with the bag should be warmer. This is the greenhouse effect. Some gases keep the heat of the sun in the atmosphere and prevent heat from escaping into space. Without the greenhouse effect Earth would be frozen and barren.

☺ ☻ **EXPLORATION: Climate Map**
There are some broad swaths of climate types on Earth. Print out the Climate Map from the end of this unit and color by number.

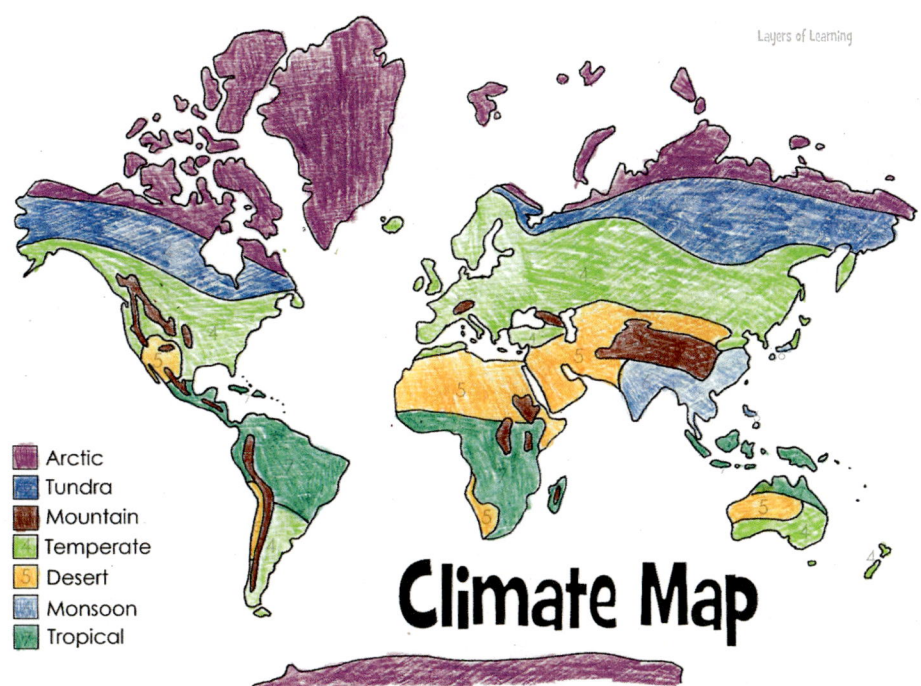

Additional Layer
Some ancient civilizations, like the Inca, worshiped the sun and knew the movement of the sun's path through the sky intimately. They knew exactly where the shadows would fall on any given day at any given time, setting up standing stones that would cast their shadows just right on an important feast day.

Fabulous Fact
Sunspots are dark spots in the surface of the sun. They are areas that are cooler than the rest of the sun. The number of sunspots increases and decreases cyclically over an 11 year period. Some scientists think sunspots are related to the overall weather patterns on Earth, like the amount of rain and the overall temperature of the earth.

Microclimates
The map to the left doesn't show the temperate rain forest on the south coast of the Caspian Sea or the alpine tundra in the northern Rockies. It also doesn't show the area in a garden that is 2 or 3 degrees warmer because it is backed by a south facing wall. These are all microclimates.

Byzantines – Turkey – Climate & Seasons – Byzantine Art

Additional Layer

Hurricane seasons can be devastating for some parts of the world. Have you ever wondered about how we name hurricanes?

Hurricanes used to be designated by latitude-longitude, which was a great way for meteorologists to track them. In 1953, the National Weather Service picked up on the habit of naval meteorologists who named storms after women. Ships were always referred to as female, and were often given women's names. In 1979, male names were inserted to alternate with the female names.

There are actually six lists of names in use for storms in the Atlantic. These lists rotate, one each year; the list of this year's names will not be reused for six years. The names get recycled each time the list comes up, with one exception: storms so devastating that reusing the name is inappropriate. So what happens if we have more storms in a year than there are names on the list? We go to the Greek alphabet – Storm Alpha, Storm Beta, and so on.

☺ ☻ ☻ **EXPLORATION: Seasonal Celebrations**

People often celebrate the coming of new seasons. Depending on which season it is, hold your own celebration.

- A garden party, bonfire, picnic, or rain dance brings in spring or summer.
- A harvest festival or feast celebrates fall and the bounty of the garden harvest.
- Many winter festivals center around the winter solstice, the shortest day of the year.

☺ ☻ ☻ **EXPERIMENT: El Niño and La Niña**

El Niño is an example of how large an effect the oceans have on weather climates. During normal weather patterns the jet stream (main weather flow patterns around the globe) flows from the Pacific Ocean over the central United States. But during an El Niño year, the water in the Pacific Ocean near the equator off the coast of South America is abnormally warm. This causes the jet stream to shift to the north. A shift like this causes havoc in the weather patterns. There will be more hurricanes, tornadoes, heavier snows, and wetter summers. In Australia and Southeast Asia there will be droughts.

The opposite effect, La Niña, occurs when the water in the Pacific off the coast of South America is cooler than usual. When that happens, droughts occur in North and South America and Australia and Southeast Asia get hammered with storms.

To show this effect you need a baking dish, hot water, cold water, a hair dryer, and food coloring.

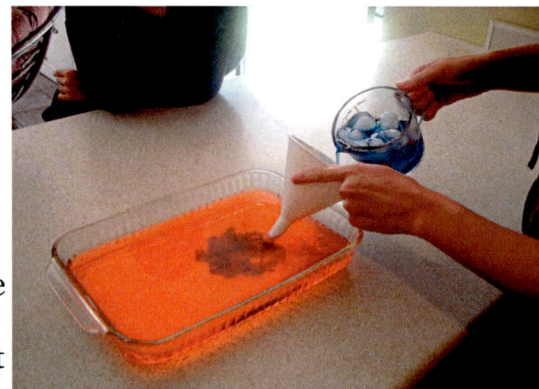

1. Get some very hot water and pour into the baking dish. Put red food coloring into the water and mix it in.
2. Now get some very cold water. Use ice to cool it way down. Add some blue food coloring.
3. Put a funnel into the hot water in the pan and very carefully add the cold water. The cold water will stay below the warm water.
4. Now turn on the hairdryer and blow a stream of air across the water. You will see hot water well up at one point and the cold water fill the other side.

BYZANTINES – TURKEY – CLIMATE & SEASONS – BYZANTINE ART

This is similar to what happens in the oceans. A warm spot of ocean water oscillates, or moves, from the waters near Indonesia (a normal year) to the waters off South America (an el Niño year). Scientists aren't sure why this happens and they don't know how to predict when it will.

Color the El Niño Weather Pattern worksheet you will find at the end of this unit.

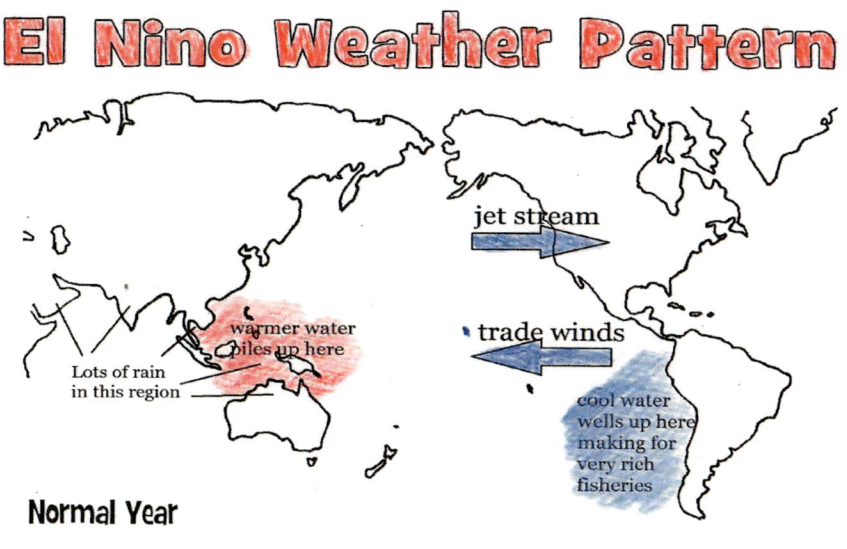

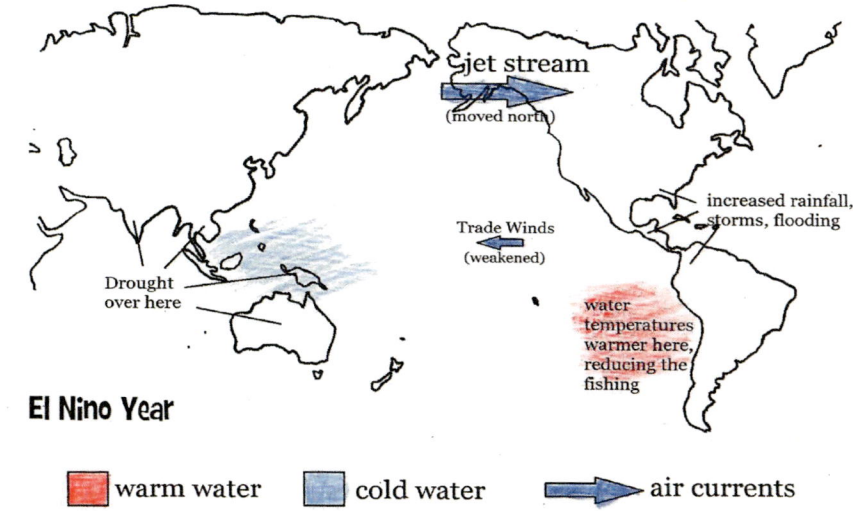

On the map you can see the trade winds in a normal year are very strong and blow in the region near the equator. They are actually so strong that the water around Australia and Indonesia literally piles up. It is several meters deeper than the water along the South American coast. In an el Niño year the trade winds drop, or sometimes even reverse direction. The ocean levels drop too, sometimes exposing and killing huge swaths of coral reefs.

The Sky Is Falling!

Some people say that whether we know if man-caused global warming is true or not, we should take steps just in case it is true.

What steps do governments (and people who try to influence governments) want to take? Are those steps harmless or do they have costs? How important is the decision of whether to "do something" about global warming? Find out.

Additional Layer

The first to observe the el Niño effect were Peruvian and Chilean fishermen along the coast of South America. They knew when the warmer water moved in they might as well pack up their nets and head home. They called it el Niño because it always happened right around Christmastime, so "el Niño" actually refers to the Christ child.

Byzantines – Turkey – Climate & Seasons – Byzantine Art

Memorization Station

The seasons change
Four times a year,
From spring to winter
They appear.

Spring is wet.
The flowers grow.
It rains a lot
And melts the snow.

Summer is hot.
It's full of sun.
There is no school.
It's lots of fun.

Fall is cool.
The leaves fall down.
The colors change
All over town.

Winter is cold,
The snowflakes fall.
We skate and ski
And make snowballs.

The seasons change
From sun to snow
And that is all
You need to know.

☺ ☻ EXPERIMENT: Why Do Leaves Change Color?

In autumn we watch leaves turn from green to yellow, orange, or red. . . why? Try this experiment:

Gather together: 5 spinach leaves, a jar, a spoon, nail polish remover, a coffee filter, some scissors, tape, and a pencil.

First, tear up the spinach leaves into little pieces and put them into the jar. Use the spoon to really mash them up well; you can even use your blender if you want to really gunge them up. Now add 3 tsp. of nail polish remover in with your leaf mush. Give them a few minutes to let the leaves settle down to the bottom, and then add as much nail polish remover as you need to cover the leaves just slightly.

Next, cut a small rectangle out of the coffee filter (about 1" wide and long enough to reach from the top of the jar down to the nail polish remover.) Tape the filter strip to the pencil on one end, and let it dangle into the nail polish remover without touching the leaves. The pencil will rest across the mouth of the glass, keeping it up. Now just sit back and let it work for a few hours.

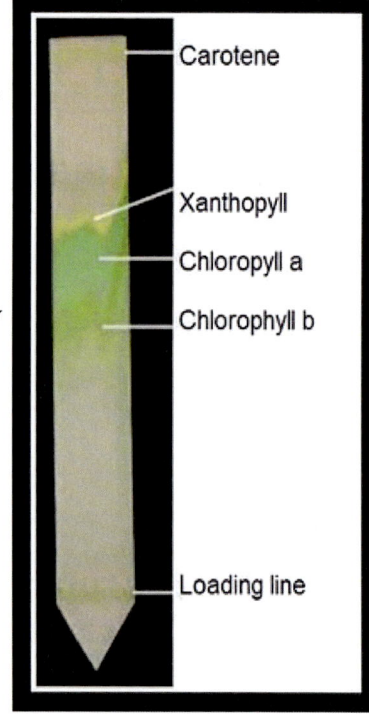

You will see colors working their way up the filter paper. The green is a chemical you've probably heard of – chlorophyll. That's what gives leaves their green color. You'll see other colors too, like reds, oranges, or yellows. These chemicals are all within green leaves too, but in the summer time when the leaves are getting lots of daylight, photosynthesis (the process by which plants turn sunlight and water into carbohydrates) provides so much chlorophyll that all we see is the green color. In the autumn less chlorophyll is produced and we begin to see the other colors that have always been hidden within the leaves.

The Arts: Byzantine Art

Byzantine artists were famous for their delicate and intricate artwork. Much of their art was religious because they were exploring Christianity and experiencing a mostly stable, peaceful time in their society. They called their works "icons" which is Greek for "images." Their religious icons were their primary expression of art.

Byzantine painters often focused on biblical scenes. Some painters believed their paintings were inspired by God. They wanted them to appear holy and dignified, with a feeling of reverence. Look over many pieces of Byzantine art and notice that very seldom will you see anyone smiling in the artwork. The images were purposely somber to show dignity. The artists also used gold leafing applied to the paintings to represent heavenly light and spirituality.

Another Byzantine art form was the mosaic. Their buildings were adorned with huge, intricate mosaic murals. In a mosaic, a picture is made up of smaller shapes pieced together to form a picture. Often the shapes are created from tile, glass, terracotta, or pebbles and pressed into plaster.

Delicate embroidery was another of their trademarks. They adorned their clothes by embroidering patterns on them with tiny stitches. Embroidered fabrics, trim pieces, and decorative patches were an essential part of their clothing. They

Additional Layer

The Hagia Sophia is a landmark in the city of Istanbul, once called Constantinople (and also called Byzantium before that). There are many architectural structures around the world that are associated with the cities they're in. The Eiffel Tower in Paris is one. Can you think of some others?

Fabulous Fact

The interior of the Hagia Sophia has many mosaics. Here is one of Jesus Christ with a halo.

Byzantines – Turkey – Climate & Seasons – Byzantine Art

Famous Folks

Kassia was an abbess, poet, and composer who lived between approximately 810 and 865 AD in Byzantium. She founded a convent near Constantinople and spent her days in study, poetry, and music. She wrote many hymns, some of which are still sung in the Eastern Orthodox church services. Her music is some of the oldest known in the world.

Additional Layer

Besides being used in art, gold leafing is sometimes used in food too! Usually as a decoration on a fancy dessert.

Pure gold is safe to eat because it's inert, but make sure before you try it that it's PURE. It should be marked edible.

frequently used geometric patterns and shapes. Flowers and birds were also popular designs. They often used bright, colorful threads to make their garments look rich.

☺ ☺ ☻ EXPLORATION: Holy Halos

Byzantine artists showed holiness by placing halos around the people they painted. The halos were simple circles surrounding the heads of the painted subjects. Often they were priests or other religious leaders, but any righteous person could be portrayed with a halo.

Make your own halo picture. Make a simple portrait of a person's head, and then surround it with a round halo. It will be particularly striking if you use dark construction paper and bright colorful chalks for the portrait, with a white or yellow chalk halo.

☺ ☻ EXPLORATION: Gold Leafing

Applying gold leaf to a whole picture is really easy. You need to get a picture you like, then have a color photocopy of it made on to a transparency sheet. If you don't have a color laser printer you'll need to take it to a copy center.

You'll need spray adhesive, gold leafing (most craft stores carry this), and a picture frame. Next, spray a tiny bit of spray adhesive on to the back of the transparency. Carefully wrinkle the gold leaf a bit so it has a crumpled look, then stick it down to the adhesive. You can use as many gold leaf pieces as you need; just make sure the whole picture gets covered.

Put it in a picture frame and you've got beautiful gold leaf art.

☺ ☻ EXPLORATION: Metal Leafing

You can use aluminum foil to add metallic details to a piece of art. You could do a metallic silhouette like the Byzantines did, or choose another subject. Here's one we did one based on one of

Byzantines – Turkey – Climate & Seasons – Byzantine Art

our favorite books, *Rainbow Fish*, by Marcus Pfister. We used a coffee filter and watercolor paints with foil, all stuck down to blue construction paper.

☺ ☻ **EXPLORATION: Miniature Mosaics**
Gather these supplies to make your own mini mosaic: a plastic container (like a plastic margarine tub), pencil and paper, mosaic pieces (you can use mosaic tiles, colored beads, broken dishes, marbles, colored glass, or stones), plaster of Paris, water, a bucket, and a paint stirrer.

Mosaics are made by pressing small decorative pieces into wet plaster. As the plaster hardens the pieces become permanently affixed to the plaster. Floors, walls, and even whole buildings have been decorated with mosaics.

First, turn the plastic container upside down and trace the circumference on to the sheet of paper. This is a template to help you lay out your design. Arrange your mosaic pieces however you'd like onto the paper inside your circle, either into a geometric or realistic design.

Next, mix the plaster in the bucket according to the package directions. Pour the plaster into the plastic container until it's

Fabulous Fact

The halos done with gold leafing around the heads of Mary and baby Jesus represent holiness.

Additional Layer

Dark blue was a popular color for art in the Byzantine world. Mary and Jesus were usually shown wearing dark blue or purple robes. Here is a Byzantine tile ceiling mosaic from Ravena, Italy.

BYZANTINES – TURKEY – CLIMATE & SEASONS – BYZANTINE ART

Writer's Workshop

The purpose of Byzantine art was to glorify the Christian religion and to put its mystery on display. The paintings of the Byzantines are full of spiritual symbolism-- things on earth are meant to stand for the higher things of heaven.

Write a journal entry about what you think the purpose of art is for you personally.

Fabulous Facts

Mosaics were often made up of several million pieces!

Mosaic pieces were set at different angles so the sun would catch the light from all directions.

Artisans also applied gold leafing over some of the tessarae to make them shine. Bold colors and a flashy appearance were definitely a trademark of Byzantine artists.

about halfway full. Allow the plaster to begin to set up a bit. When it feels like soft clay, arrange the design as you planned it on the paper. Start in the middle and work your way out to the edges. Work quickly so the plaster won't dry before you're finished.

When you're done let it dry for an hour, separate the sides of the container from the plaster, then place a soft rag over the top and dump it out carefully. If it begins to crack it needs to dry a bit longer.

🙂 🟢 EXPLORATION: Paper Mosaics

Use torn or cut paper bits and glue them down to craft paper to make your own paper mosaic design.

🟢 EXPLORATION: Bean Mosaics

Use a piece of cardboard or a heavy paper plate as your base. Sketch your outlined design on the cardboard, then fill in sections with glue, sticking beans down as you go. You can create any picture or design you'd like. You can use any kinds of dry beans, rice, or pasta noodles.

If you want more or brighter colors, use jelly beans to create your mosaic.

Byzantines – Turkey – Climate & Seasons – Byzantine Art

😊 🙂 EXPLORATION: Foam Square Mosaics

You can purchase template designs or just buy sticky foam shapes and combine them to make your own pictures. Use cardboard or heavy card stock as your base page so it will be sturdy enough for the foam shapes. These mosaics are faster than dealing with glue for each tile, so your designs can easily be more intricate. They are much less messy and sticky too!

😊 🙂 EXPEDITION: Embroidery How-To

Try out this virtual expedition if you don't know how to embroider. Go visit Needle 'n Thread at www.needlenthread.com to learn hand embroidery stitches. A variety of how-to videos demonstrate lots of different stitches. They also provide lots of simple printable patterns.

The easiest type of embroidery is cross stitch. Black and red cross stitch patterns are typical of eastern Europe, formerly Byzantine lands.

This embroidery was done by Paula Kate Marmor, CC license

Fabulous Fact

This is a mosaic of the famous Byzantine Emperor, Justinian. The mosaic picture or design is made of thousands of small glass or marble cubes, called tesserae, set in cement. The walls and domes of the great churches of Ravenna and Constantinople were decorated with brilliantly colored glass tesserae.

Fabulous Fact

The Byzantines often put gold leafing behind clear glass tessarae so they would shine.

Writer's Workshop

Often people embroider meaningful poems, quotes, or scriptures to hang on their walls to serve as inspiration art.

If you could have any poem, quote, or scripture embroidered for your wall, what would you choose? Why?

Write about and why it inspires you in your writer's notebook.

Byzantines – Turkey – Climate & Seasons – Byzantine Art

Additional Layer

Read Exodus 20:4 from the Bible. Old Testament prohibitions against worshiping graven images provided one of the most important precedents for Byzantine iconoclasm.

Writer's Workshop

Censoring artwork and literature is still a hot topic today. Do some research about it and then write an opinion essay about your point of view on the issue.

😊 😊 😊 EXPEDITION: Virtual Hagia Sophia Tour

Take an armchair tour of the Hagia Sofia, Byzantium's famous cathedral built by Justinian.
http://www.360tr.com/34_istanbul/ayasofya/english/
This site is a 360 degree video tour; it's awesome, and the next best thing to actually going there.

😊 😊 😊 EXPLORATION: Solemnity

Fold a sheet of paper in half and then draw a line along the fold line so your paper is bisected. On one side, draw a picture of your family, friends, or others you know well. Make it represent the way you see them. It can be a full-body sketch or just their faces.

Once you're done, draw the same picture on the second half, except use the solemnity of the Byzantines. No one should be smiling or look happy. They should have very solemn (though not necessarily sad) expressions. This was the way the Byzantines showed dignity.

😊 😊 EXPLORATION: Image Smashers

At this time in the Byzantine Empire the church leaders fought about the artwork. Some thought that the beautiful, religious art could help teach the gospel, especially at a time when many people couldn't read. Others though, believed that the art had become idols and that people were worshiping the art instead of God. They were called iconoclasts, or image smashers. Through much of Byzantium, religious art was completely banned. Most icons were destroyed, so we don't have very many of them in existence today.

Discuss what you think about this idea. What purpose does religious art serve? Are there valid reasons to destroy artwork?

Coming up next . . .

Unit 2-2

Barbarians – Ireland
Forecasting
Illuminated Art

Byzantines – Turkey – Climate & Seasons – Byzantine Art

My Ideas For This Unit:

Title: _____ Topic: _____

_____
_____
_____
_____
_____
_____
_____
_____
_____

Title: _____ Topic: _____

_____
_____
_____
_____
_____
_____
_____
_____
_____

Title: _____ Topic: _____

_____
_____
_____
_____
_____
_____
_____
_____

BYZANTINES – TURKEY – CLIMATE & SEASONS – BYZANTINE ART

My Ideas For This Unit:

Title: _____ Topic: _____

_____
_____
_____
_____
_____
_____
_____
_____
_____

Title: _____ Topic: _____

_____
_____
_____
_____
_____
_____
_____
_____
_____

Title: _____ Topic: _____

_____
_____
_____
_____
_____
_____
_____
_____
_____

The Byzantine Empire

The Byzantine Empire was really the Eastern Roman Empire, which survived for a thousand years after the Western Roman Empire fell. Emperor Justinian was the greatest of the Byzantine Emperors. He conquered land that greatly expanded the size of the empire and wrote a law code that is still the basis of much western law.

Byzantine Empire: Unit 2-1

330 AD 2-1
Constantine makes Byzantium his capital and renames it Constantinople

527 AD 2-1

Justinian becomes emperor of the Eastern Roman Empire

639 AD 2-1
Muslim armies conquer southern lands of the empire: Syria, Holy Land, Egypt, Jordan

726 AD 2-1

Emperor Leo III orders all icons (religious paintings) destroyed

843 AD 2-1
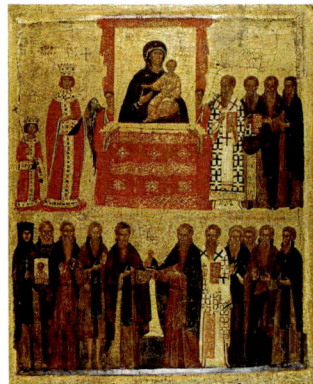
Icons restored by Empress Theodora

1054 AD 2-1
The Patriarch in Constantinople and the Pope in Rome excommunicate one another, splitting the church

1071 AD 2-1

Seljuk Turks defeat Byzantines and take Asia Minor

1081 AD 2-1

Byzantium defeats an attack from the Norman state of South Italy

1204 AD 2-1
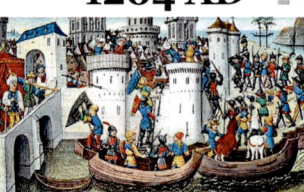
4th Crusade; Crusaders occupy Constantinople and sack the city

1261 AD 2-1

Constantinople is recaptured by Byzantine Emperor, Michael Palaeologus

1300-1450 AD 2-1

Byzantine Empire slowly loses land to the Turks until the city Constantinople stands alone

1453 AD 2-1

Ottoman Turks take Constantinople

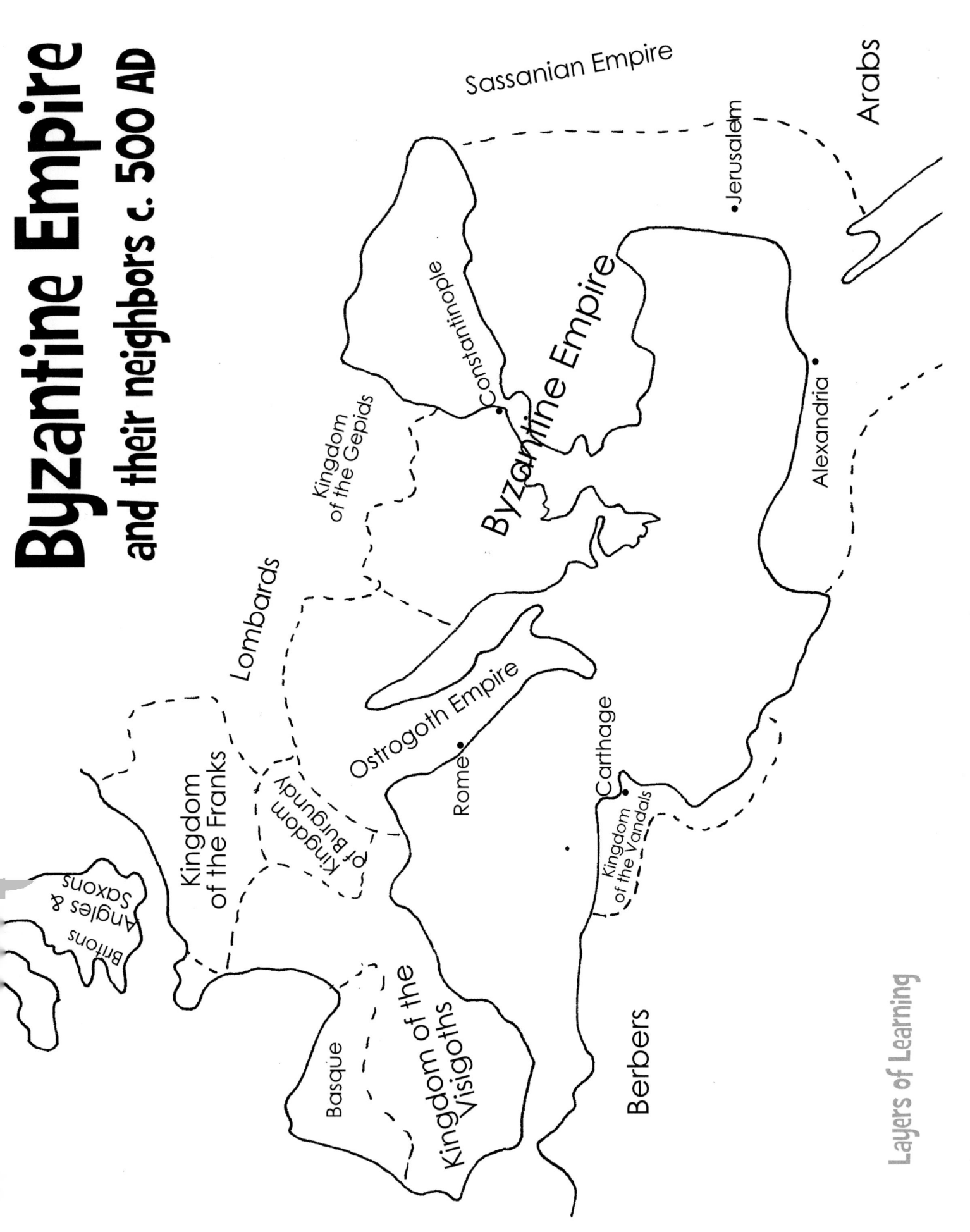

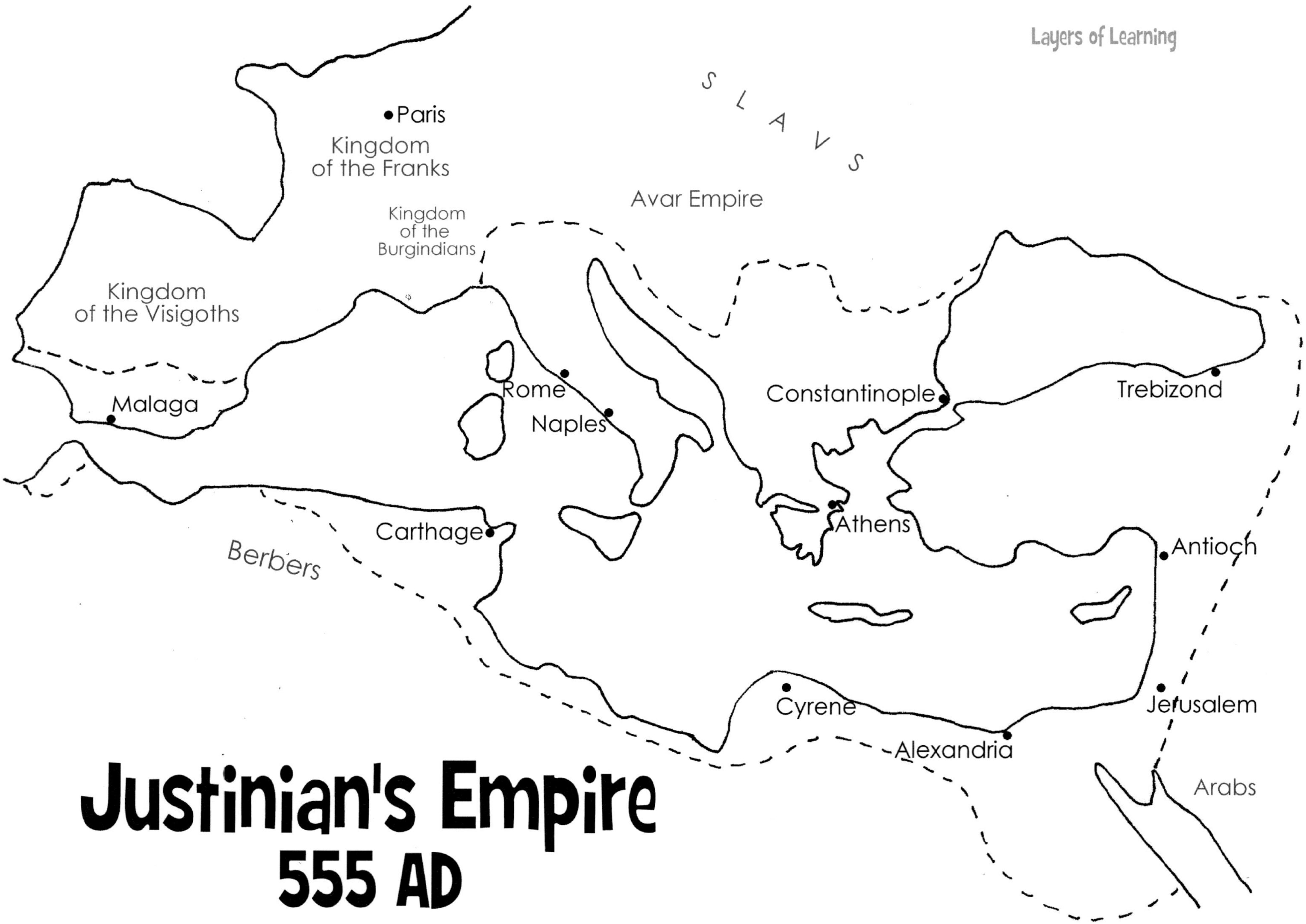

Justinian's Empire 555 AD

Layers of Learning

- Trebizond
- Antioch
- Jerusalem
- Arabs
- Constantinople
- Athens
- Cyrene
- Alexandria
- SLAVS
- Avar Empire
- Rome
- Naples
- Paris
- Kingdom of the Franks
- Kingdom of the Burgundians
- Carthage
- Berbers
- Kingdom of the Visigoths
- Malaga

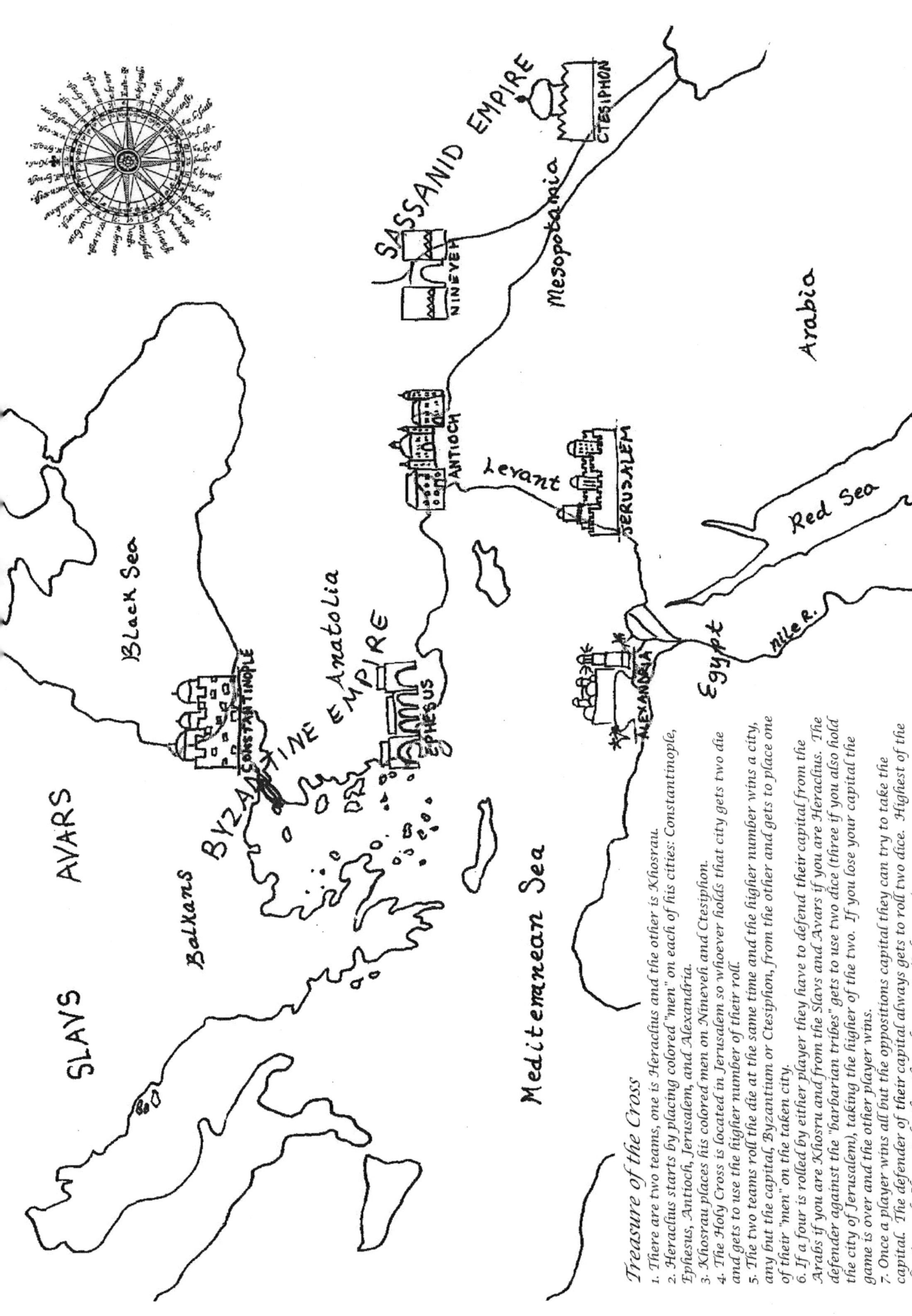

Treasure of the Cross

1. There are two teams, one is Heraclius and the other is Khosrau.
2. Heraclius starts by placing colored "men" on each of his cities: Constantinople, Ephesus, Antioch, Jerusalem, and Alexandria.
3. Khosrau places his colored men on Nineveh and Ctesiphon.
4. The Holy Cross is located in Jerusalem so whoever holds that city gets two die and gets to use the higher number of their roll.
5. The two teams roll the die at the same time and the higher number wins a city, any but the capital, Byzantium or Ctesiphon, from the other and gets to place one of their "men" on the taken city.
6. If a four is rolled by either player they have to defend their capital from the Arabs if you are Khosru and from the Slavs and Avars if you are Heraclius. The defender against the "barbarian tribes" gets to use two dice (three if you also hold the city of Jerusalem), taking the higher of the two. If you lose your capital the game is over and the other player wins.
7. Once a player wins all but the oppositions capital they can try to take the capital. The defender of their capital always gets to roll two dice. Highest of the dice is used. If you take the other players capital you win.
8. One more rule. All tie rolls go to Khorasan, because he starts with fewer cities or to the defender if it is vs. the Barbarian Tribes.

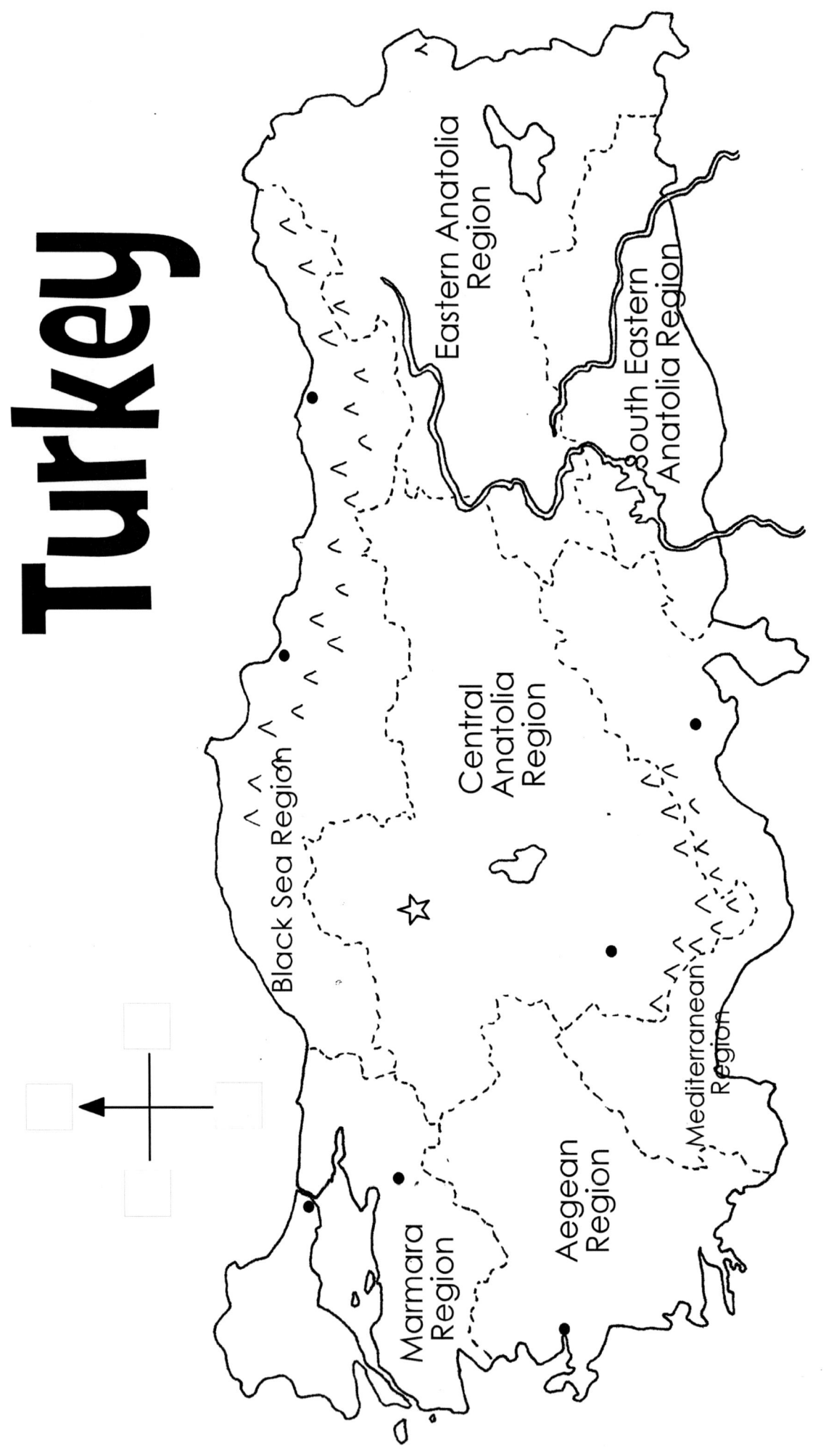

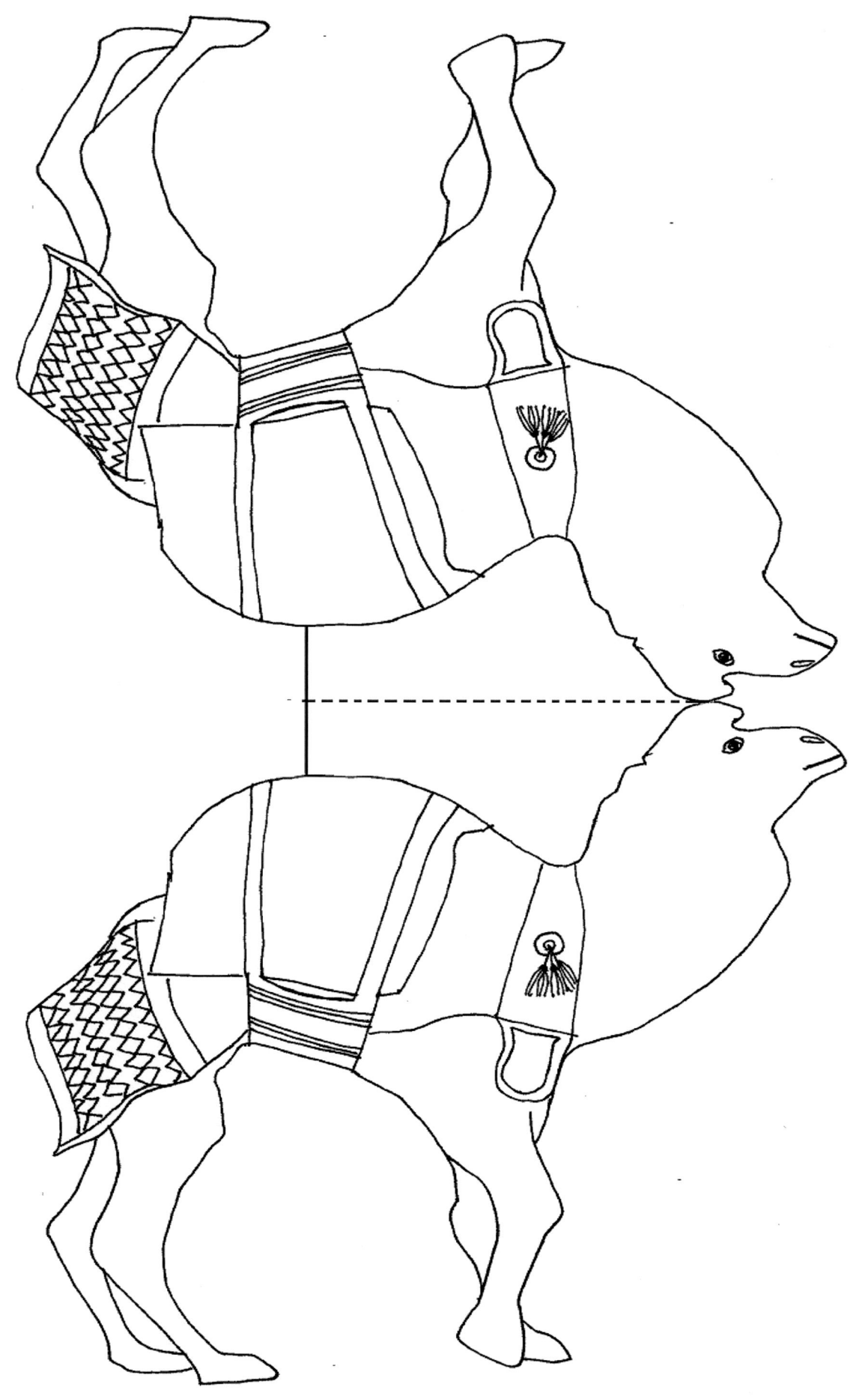

Flag of Turkey

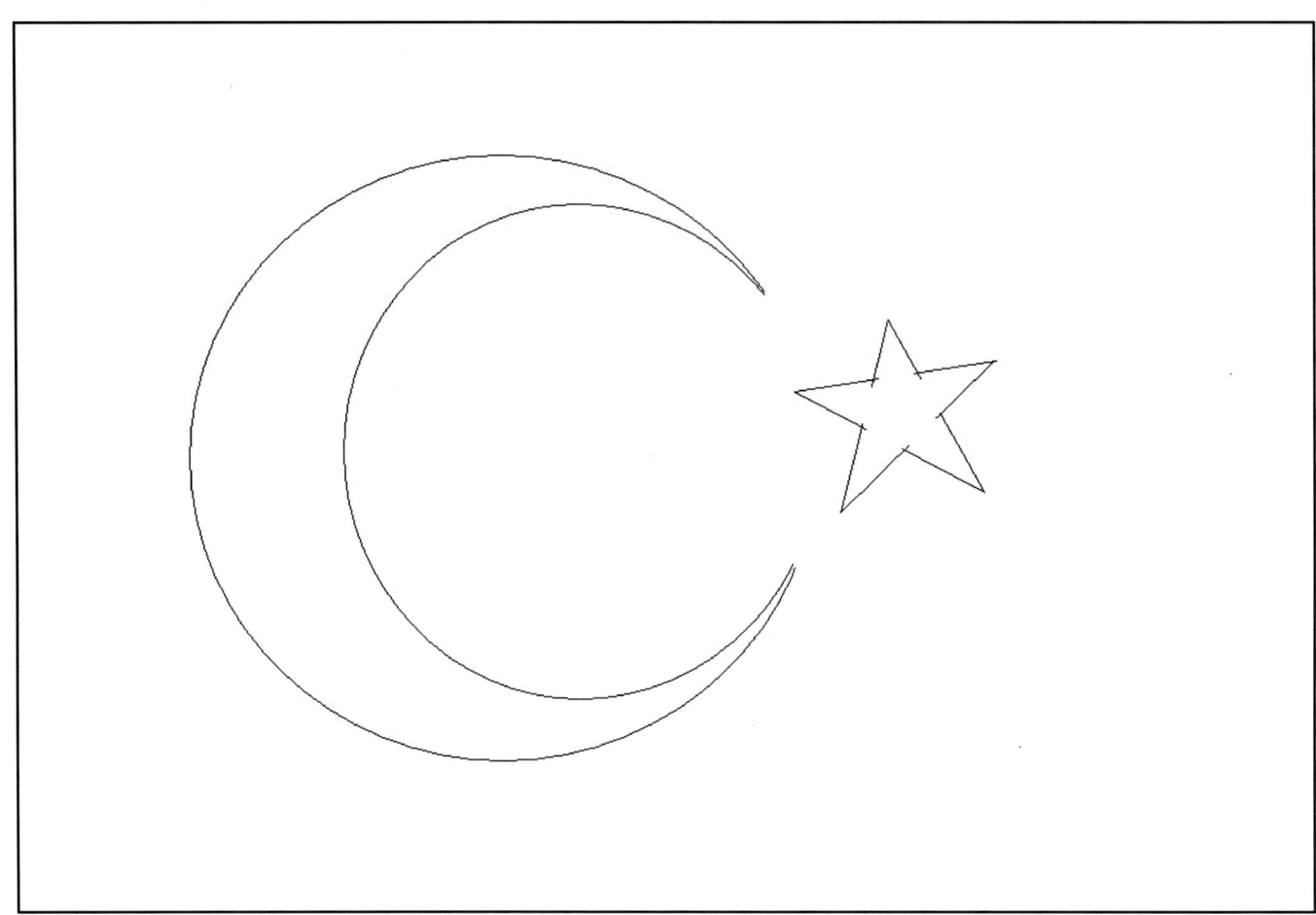

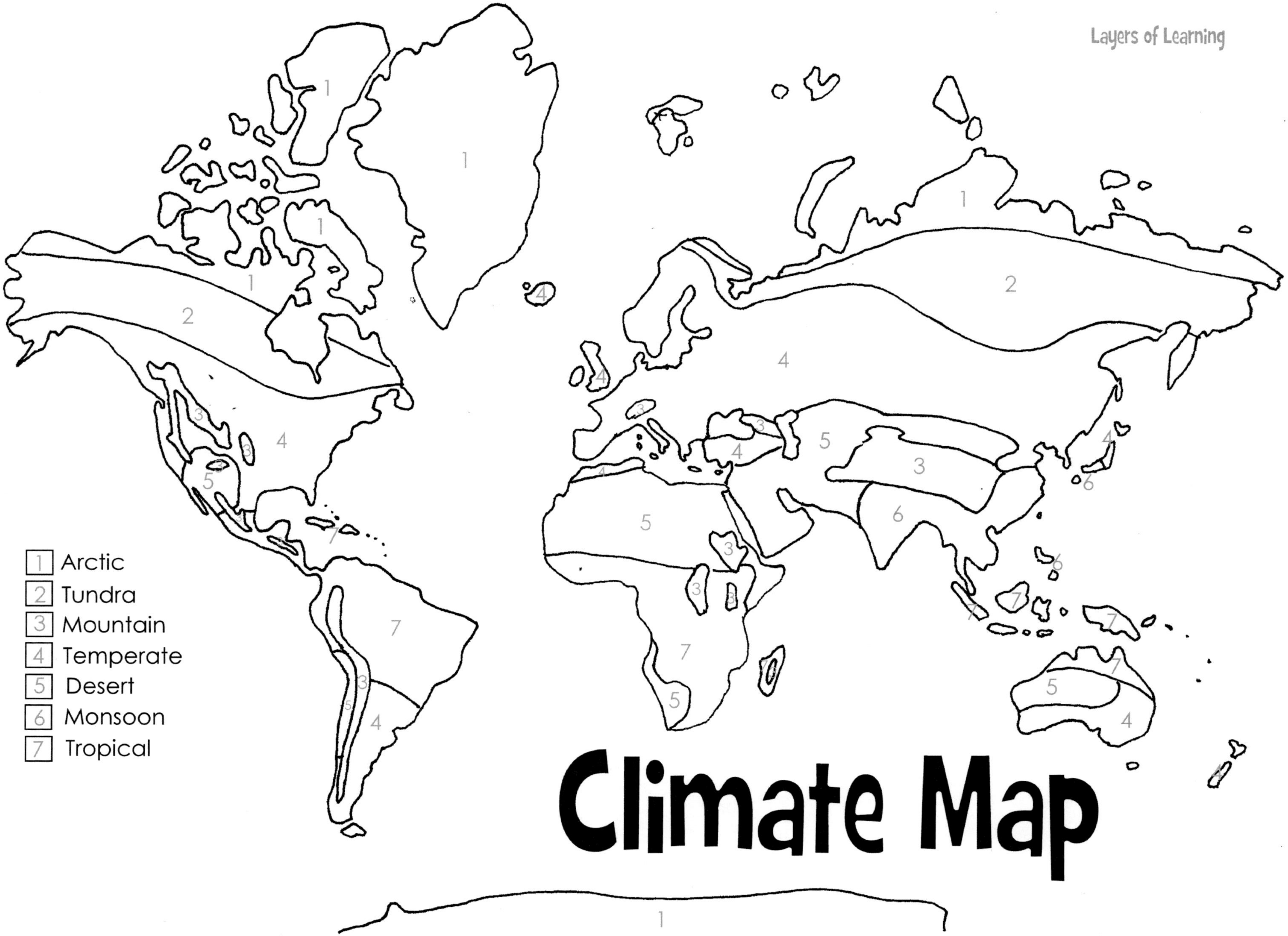

Climate Map

Layers of Learning

1. Arctic
2. Tundra
3. Mountain
4. Temperate
5. Desert
6. Monsoon
7. Tropical

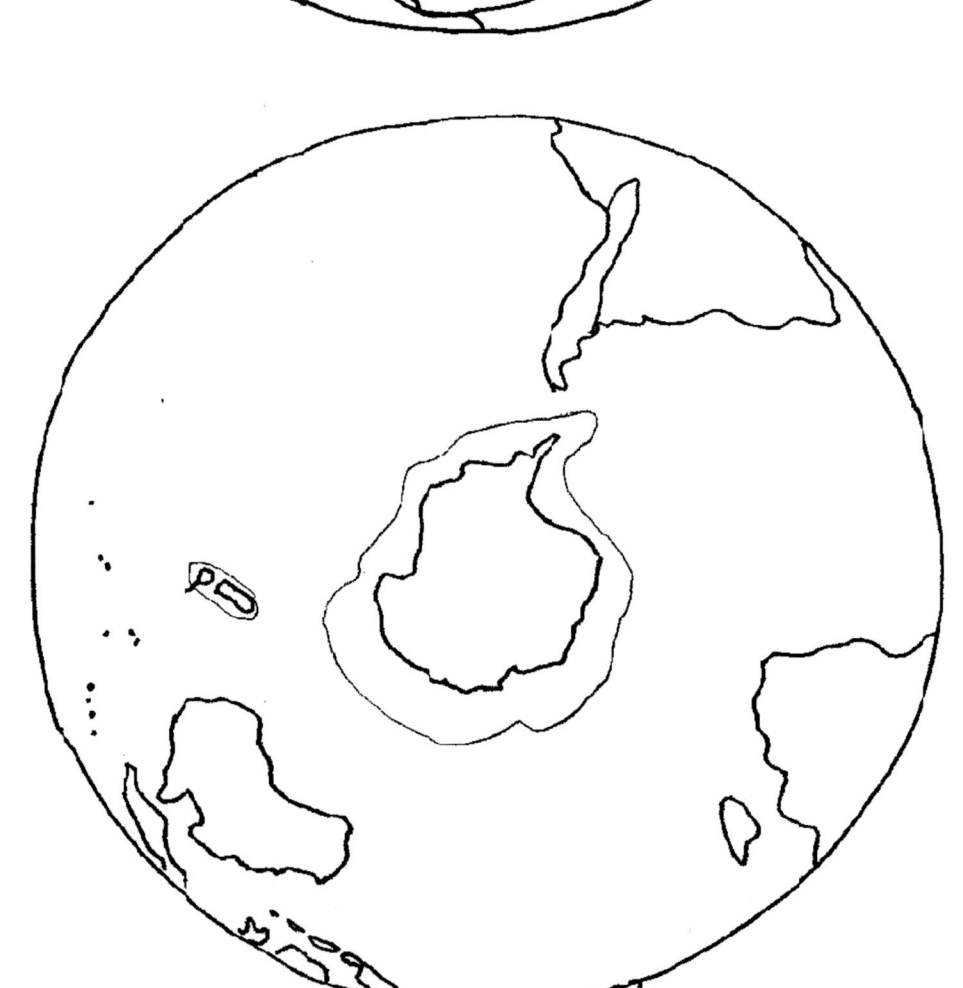

Global Climate Change

☐ Extent of polar ice caps and ice sheets today

☐ Extent of polar ice caps and ice sheets during the last ice age

Northern Hemisphere

Southern Hemisphere

El Nino Weather Pattern

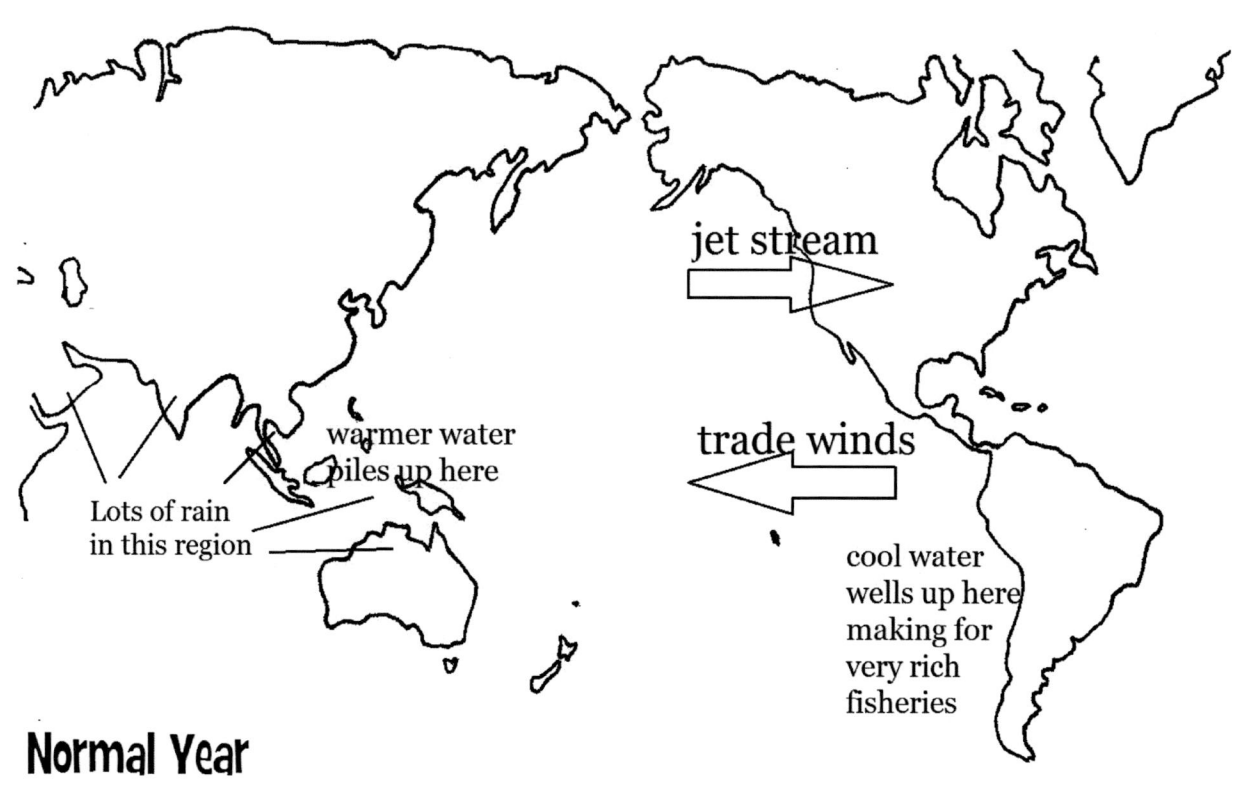

Normal Year

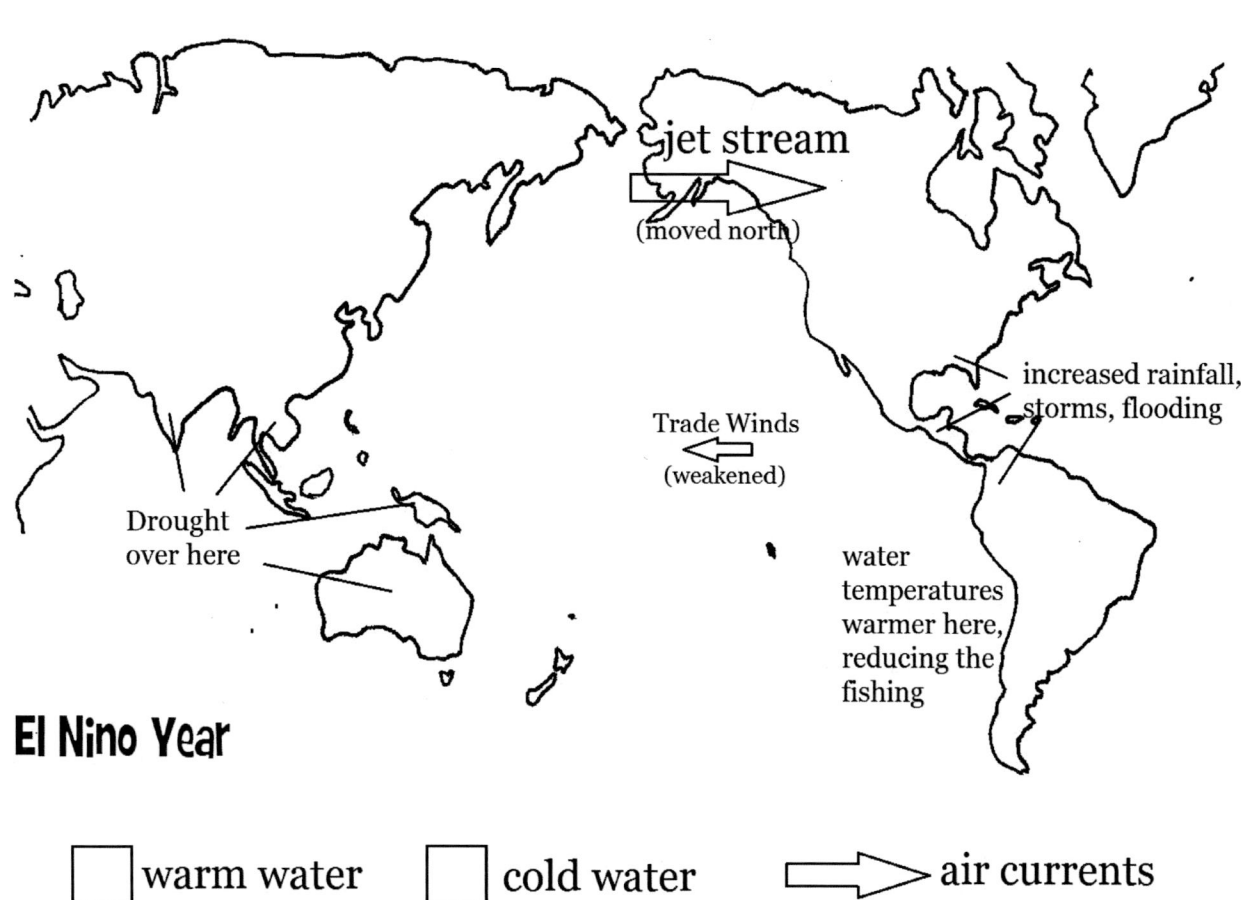

El Nino Year

About the Authors

Karen & Michelle . . .
Mothers, sisters, teachers, women who are passionate
about educating kids.
We are dedicated to lifelong learning.

Karen, a mother of four, who has homeschooled her kids for more than eight years with her husband, Bob, has a bachelor's degree in child development with an emphasis in education. She lives in Utah where she gardens, teaches piano, and plays an excruciating number of board games with her kids. Karen is our resident Arts expert and English guru {most necessary as Michelle regularly and carelessly mangles the English language and occasionally steps over the bounds of polite society}.

Michelle and her husband, Cameron, homeschooling now for over a decade, teach their six boys on their ten acres in beautiful Idaho country. Michelle earned a bachelor's in biology, making her the resident Science expert, though she is mocked by her friends for being the *Botanist with the Black Thumb of Death*. She also is the go-to for History and Government. She believes in staying up late, hot chocolate, and a no whining policy. We both pitch in on Geography, in case you were wondering, and are on a continual quest for knowledge.

*Visit our constantly updated blog for tons of free ideas,
free printables, and more cool stuff for sale:*
www.Layers-of-Learning.com

Made in the USA
San Bernardino, CA
19 October 2018